LAURELS FOR
PRINZ WITTGENSTEIN

By

Werner P. Roell

Published in 1994 by
Independent Books
3 Leaves Green Crescent
Keston
Bromley BR2 6DN
Great Britain

First published in 1993 by v. Hase & Koehler Verlag, Mainz

Entitled: 'Blumen für Prinz Wittgenstein'

ISBN 3-7758-1279-2

Translated from the original German by Bob Walter

This edition by Independent Books

ISBN 1-872836-06-2

Printed and bound by Bookcraft (Bath) Ltd.

A catalogue record for this book is available from the British Library

CONTENTS

PHOTOGRAPHS AND ILLUSTRATIONS

THE AUTHOR

Werner P. Roell was born in France in 1914, the son of German parents. In 1934 he became an Officer Cadet in the German Navy for employment as an airman. The following year he attended Flying Training Schools at Salzwedel and Schleissheim, near Munich. He was promoted to *Leutnant* in the *Main Geschwader* in 1936 and undertook fighter and dive bomber (Stuka) training, then moving on to the War College.

During World War II he flew 477 operations against the enemy in Norway, Yugoslavia, Crete and Russia, being awarded the *Ritterkreuz* (Knight's Cross) for Stuka operations against shipping, tanks and bridges.

In 1945, at the end of the war, he served with *Jagdverband* Galland at Riem/Munich where, on 9 April after an American daylight raid on Munich, he saved a young American airman, who had bailed out, from being shot.

After the end of the war Werner worked as an interpreter and from 1948 to 1952 as a sports master at the German School in Santiago/Chile. In 1953 he returned to Germany to begin building up an engineering works but maintained a link with the military by taking reserve training as an *Oberstleutnant* in the Attaché Service. Werner P. Roell is married and has four children. His hobbies are writing and painting.

ACKNOWLEDGEMENTS

Robert Bossard - *'The Psychology of Dreams'*, Martin Middlebrook - *'The Berlin Raids-RAF Bomber Command Winter 1943/44'*, Alexander McKee - *'Dresden 1945 - The Devil's Tinderbox'* (Souvenir Press 1982), Basil Collier - *'The Defence of the United Kingdom'* (HMSO 1957). Marie Vassilitchikov - *'Berlin Diaries, 1940 - 1945'*.

TRANSLATOR'S NOTES

The following note was not originally penned by Bob Walter, the translator of this book. But, because it so succinctly expresses the substance and problems of the translation of a German military book to English it is used here by kind permission of the original author.

I have, as far as seems to me to be reasonable, used the original German designations for ranks and for units. For those unfamiliar with them, I have listed below the nearest equivalent ranks in both the Royal Air Force and the United States Air Force. Any possible slight misunderstandings between ranks and functions (a *Kapitän*, for example, is not a Captain but a leader of a *Staffel*) should be clarified readily by the context. I believe that to try to anglicise robs works such as this of much of their atmosphere.

The case for keeping to the original designations of units is very strong, in that there were no direct equivalents between those of the *Luftwaffe* and those of the Allied Air Forces. In the explanation that I now give, I am speaking in general terms, and the reader should bear in mind that there were variations to the general rule.

The basic flying unit of the *Luftwaffe* was the *Staffel*, which usually comprised nine aircraft: it was commanded by a junior officer, normally an *Oberleutnant* or a *Hauptmann*. He was the *Kapitän*, or, to give him his full title, the *Staffelkapitän*. The number of aircrew in a *Staffel* varied according to the type of aircraft it operated: clearly more flying personnel were needed for a *Staffel* of He 111 bombers than for a *Staffel* of Bf 109 fighters. A *Gruppe*, the next higher unit, originally contained thirty aircraft, made up of three *Staffeln* (I will speak of German plurals below) plus a Staff or Headquarters Flight *(Stabsschwarm)* of three machines. The commanding officer of a *Gruppe* was usually a *Major*, sometimes a *Hauptmann*, and he was the *Kommandeur* or *Gruppenkommandeur*.

Moving yet higher - to the largest flying unit - we come to the *Geschwader*, usually made up of three *Gruppen* - ninety aircraft - plus a *Stabsschwarm* of four, making ninety-four machines in all. It was commanded by an *Oberst*, an *Oberstleutnant* or a *Major*, who was the *Geschwaderkommodore*, or simply *Kommodore*.

Geschwader of all functions - bombers, fighters, dive bombers, reconnaissance aircraft and so on - were incorporated in *Luftflotten (Luftflotte* = Air Fleet). Each *Luftflotte* was in practice an independent air force and was deployed geographically. In 1943, for example, *Luftflotte 3* covered the Low Countries and Southern Germany, and *Luftflotte 2* covered Northern Germany.

In overall control of the Luftwaffe was the *Reichsluftfahrtministerium* (RLM), or *Reich* Ministry of Aviation [the Germans tend to string their individual words together to make up longer words - the RLM contains the words *Reich*, *Luft* (Air), *Fahrt* (Travel), and *Ministerium* (Ministry)].The RLM was responsible for both military and civil flying matters. Its Head, Hermann Göring, had the dual responsibility of Commander-in-Chief of the Air Force (*Oberbefehlshaber der Luftwaffe*) and *Reich* Minister of Aviation *(Reichsminister der Luftfahrt)*.

Other elements of the military aviation organisation of the Third Reich were the *Luftgau* (a 'Gau' being an administrative district) and the *Fliegerkorps*. The geographical area covered by each *Luftflotte* was divided into a number of *Luftgaue*, which were responsible for administration, supply, airfield personnel and some aircraft servicing for the airfields within their area. The *Fliegerkorps* was the parallel organisation responsible for all organisational matters.

Unit designations within the *Luftwaffe* were abbreviated: K = *Kampf* (Bomber); J = *Jagd* (Fighter); NJ - *Nachtjagd* (Night Fighter); and so on. To translate *Jagd* as 'Fighter', as I have done above, is inaccurate. Correctly, *Jagd* translates as 'hunting' or 'the hunt', and what we would call a fighter, a *Jäger*, as a 'hunter' or 'huntsman'. The hunting ethic was very strong in Germany and Göring was a passionate hunter: *Wilde Sau* fits nicely into this concept. More about *Wilde Sau* below. To revert to the naming of units: KG was a *Kampfgeschwader*, JG a *Jagdgeschwader*, NJG a *Nachtjagdgeschwader*, and so on. Each *Geschwader* had a number, for instance KG 4. The number of the *Gruppe*, in Roman numerals, preceded the *Geschwader* number, so IV./KG 3 was the Fourth *Gruppe* of *Kampfgeschwader* No 3. Individual *Staffeln* had their own numbers, and these in contrast to those of *Gruppen*, were shown in Arabic numerals. *5./KG 4*, for example, was the 5th *Staffel* of *Kampfgeschwader* No 4. As there were three *Staffeln* to a *Gruppe*, it can readily be seen that the 5th *Staffel* belonged to the 2nd *Gruppe* (*II.KG 4*).

German plurals are not as simple as English ones. For instance, *Staffel - Staffeln, Gruppe - Gruppen, Geschwader - Geschwader, Kapitän - Kapitäne, Hauptmann - Hauptleute* (believe it or not). I hope that when I use plurals in the original German they will be identifiable readily as such from the text.

Finally, *Wilde Sau*, which I have translated as 'Wild Boar', although I would have preferred to use 'Wild Sow', the literal translation. In German, to 'behave like a wild sow' is to act madly, unheedingly, crazily. The expression has its origins in the behaviour of the female wild pig when her young are threatened, and that fits rather nicely, I think, with the concept of Göring's night-fighter pilots defending their country and their people. But 'Wild Boar' has, by now, become an accepted item of vocabulary in the history of air warfare, and I have bowed to usage.

Peter Hinchliffe OBE translator of Hajo Herrmann's excellent book 'Eagle's Wings'.

APPROXIMATE EQUIVALENT RANKS

Luftwaffe	Royal Air Force	US Air Force
Flieger	Aircraftsman	Private
Obergefreiter	LAC	Corporal
Unteroffizier	Corporal	Staff Sergeant
Feldwebel	Sergeant	Tech. Sergeant
Oberfeldwebel	Flight Sergeant	Master Sergeant
Hauptfeldwebel	Warrant Officer	Warrant Officer
Fähnrich	Officer Cadet	Officer Cadet
Leutnant	Pilot Officer	Second Lieutenant
Oberleutnant	Flying Officer	First Lieutenant
Hauptmann	Flight Lieutenant	Captain
Major	Squadron Leader	Major
Oberstleutnant	Wing Commander	Lieutenant Colonel
Oberst	Group Captain	Colonel
Generalmajor	Air Commodore	Brigadier General
Generalleutnant	Air Vice Marshal	Major General
General	Air Marshal	Lieutenant General
Generaloberst	Air Chief Marshal	Four Star General
Generalfeldmarschall	Marshal of the RAF	Five Star General

When a senior German officer was appointed to a staff job, the letters
'i. G' were added to his rank, *'i. G'* being short for *'im Generalstab'* -
'On the General Staff'. So where we have, for example, *Oberst i. G*
it has been translated as Staff *Oberst*, etc.

*For Irmela, in memory of her brother
Wolfgang, who fell in the War*

'A people which parts from its history,
and then finds shame burning its brow,
will be wiped by God from the slate.'

Johann Wolfgang von Goethe

WITH THANKS

An airman who aspires to become an Author needs such people as will take his winged horse by the rein so that it will not break away.

Such were Heidi Walkhoff and Paulheinz Grupe. They are to be thanked, as are Walburga Prinzessin Sayn-Wittgenstein, Alexander Robert Brosch, Dr Eng. Herbert Kümmritz, Friedrich Ostheimer and Jürgen Clausen, to all of whose writings I was allowed to refer.

Lake Constance, Autumn 1992   Werner P. Roell

Heinrich Prinz zu Sayn-Wittgenstein
as *Hauptmann*

FOREWORD

'There was a brilliant young German aristocrat who made an enduring mark with the *Luftwaffe* in the night skies over Germany, occupied Europe and the Eastern Front and who did, indeed, capture the public gaze. Heinrich Prinz zu Sayn-Wittgenstein's story is conspicuous for being far removed from the general run.'

When I wrote those words in 1982, I did not know that a biography of this remarkable young German officer of noble upbringing was being written. Now I rejoice, for it is right that, half a century on, with the past mercifully fading further and further into the distance, the story of Sayn-Wittgenstein should be told, if only for one reason: it will enable generations which have come after to know something of the quality of leadership which existed in each of the two air forces - the *Luftwaffe* and the Royal Air Force - in those awful years which have come to be known as the Second World War...

It is the extent of the chivalry which animated those who were leading the *Luftwaffe's Geschwader, Gruppen* and *Staffeln* and their counterparts among the Royal Air Force's groups, wings and squadrons.

The story of Sayn-Wittgenstein provides one exceptional instance of the humanity which abounded in the two great air forces.

Wing Commander P.B. 'Laddie' Lucas CBE DSO DFC
London, January 1994

UNUS PRO MULTIS

(One of many)

Autumn 1992, the day of German Unity. People have gathered in the grounds of the derelict *Bismarckschloss* in Schönhausen, between Stendal and Rathenau. There are men and women, uniformed and in civilian clothes, old and young. One can see from afar that many are soldiers, even if some are not recognisable as such from what they are wearing. In the venerable 800 year old brick-built Gothic church, the last hymn has faded and the solemn ecumenical service has come to an end.

The quiet conversations here in the park are in German, English or French. The whole scene radiates solemnity. These people have gathered round a small rock, a so-called erratic boulder, a memorial stone among flower beds, which is to be dedicated today.

A Bundeswehr platoon, young soldiers from the new *Länder*, has paraded to honour a German soldier who was killed in the Second World War, a situation which was inconceivable before German Reunification. On the right flank is the platoon commander, a lieutenant and a trumpeter. The hunting horn *ensemble* from the municipality of Schönhausen joins the soldiers.

On the stone, apart from a stylised Iron Cross, only a name, with the dates of birth and death, is carved, '*Major Heinrich Prinz zu Sayn-Wittgenstein. Unus pro Multis*'. In memory of a man who, more than 48 years ago, lost his life not far from this place of remembrance, a life out of the ordinary which ended too soon, a man out of the ordinary, who, in terms of the basic traits of his character and appearance, was outstanding and unique but who, sadly, embodied an all too typical fate of his time, and of his generation.

The great-nephew of the soldier to be honoured, and

who, again bears the name of Heinrich Prinz zu Sayn-Wittgenstein, performs the unveiling of the memorial stone.

After the trumpet solo *'Ich hatt' ein Kameraden'*, wreaths were laid on behalf of the Fighter Pilots' Association, the *Ritterkreuz* Association and of 17 Cavalry Regiment.

Thereafter the President of the Fighter Pilots' Association made a speech paying tribute to the personality of Prinz Wittgenstein, and said:

'We are gathered here today, the 3rd of October 1992, the Day of German Unity, in the grounds of the Bismarck Estate at Schönhausen, to remember *Major* Heinrich Prinz zu Sayn-Wittgenstein, *Kommodore* of *2 Nachtjagdgeschwader*, and to unveil in his honour a memorial stone which stands near the spot where he met an airman's death, following an air battle on the night of 21/22 January 1994.

On this autumn day, nearly five decades after the event, former members of night fighter units have travelled from all quarters of our Fatherland to join the last *Kommodore* of *1 Nachtjagdgeschwader, Oberstleutnant* Hans-Joachim Jabs, to show their respect and admiration for the achievements of this extraordinary personality, and, at the same time, to remember the spirit of sacrifice and the brave nightly operations of those crews who lost their lives.

The Fighter Pilots' Association feels itself dedicated to a clean and creditable tradition which excludes uncritical boasting about our past. On the basis of this commitment we have, over decades, built bridges to the fighting units of our (present day) *Luftwaffe*. We are therefore moved, in this moment of remembrance, by the participation of a Guard of Honour from the *Luftwaffe* exemplifying the closeness between the generations of airmen. The presence of the deputy commander of *5. Luftwaffen-Division,*

Brigadegeneral Günter Lange, is likewise an indication of close comradeship.

Heinrich Prinz zu Sayn-Wittgenstein was born on 14 August 1916 in Copenhagen and joined the *Luftwaffe* in 1937. He flew 150 fighter operations in the course of the campaign in the West against England and on the Eastern Front, until he transferred to night fighters in 1941. He became a prominent figure in night fighting through his eagerness for action and his dazzling ability. As a *Staffelkapitän*, as a *Gruppenkommandeur* and as a *Kommodore* he was a respected and energetic leader of outstanding quality. In the course of 170 operations against the enemy, he emerged successful from the "Duel beneath the stars" 83 times and was decorated with the Oak Leaves and Swords. With a total of 83 victories he was the most successful night fighter pilot at the time of his death. He has gone into the history of air warfare in WWII as the third most successful night fighter pilot after *Major* Heinz-Wolfgang Schnaufer (121) and *Oberst* Helmut Lent (113). These are, in brief, the biographical data of a gallant and successful air force officer with a high sense of duty whom we remember with gratitude at this hour... His personality is an example to us all, in the sense of good military tradition. With *Major* Prinz Heinrich zu Sayn-Wittgenstein, we remember all the fallen comrades who stood at our side in the difficult and cruel years of war.'

The next speaker was the Head of the House of Wittgenstein, H.H.Alexander Fürst zu Sayn-Wittgenstein who honoured his late uncle:

'We are gathered here today to honour the memory of my late uncle, the night fighter pilot Heinrich Prinz zu Sayn-Wittgenstein. We have set up a memorial stone to him near the place where his aircraft crashed.

It is certainly an unusual event to honour a dead soldier almost five decades after his death. Why are we doing this? What motivates us? Who was this man?

I had contact with Heinrich on only one occasion, at Christmas 1943, a few weeks after I was born, and a few weeks before he was killed, when he held me over the font. Only very much later did I get to know him better, when his mother told me about him.

From stories of my old, lonely grandmother, who had outlived her husband and her three sons, I felt how extraordinary her Heinrich must have been. A man, a character so full of contradictions, that I, his young nephew, who was growing up in ordered and peaceful times, was gripped by a fascination about him, without, I must confess, ever having properly understood him.

His upbringing was completely cosmopolitan, born in Denmark, domiciled in Switzerland, his grandmother a Frenchwoman, his great-grandmother, Leonilla, a Russian; he had some of his best friends and relatives in England - and yet he fought inexorably against the British, Russians and French.

He was, his mother told me, an enthusiastic member of the Hitler Youth - and yet counted among his very closest friends the young men and women who, five months after his death, on 20 July 1944, wanted to put an end to this madness.

He was delicate, almost frail - and yet, filled with burning ambition and pugnacity, was capable of superhuman achievements.

Who was Heinrich? I think that we, the young generation who had the good fortune to grow up in peace-loving times, to whom everything military was foreign, for whom the downfall of the great German Wilhelminian *Reich* lay in the dim past, who regarded the Versailles Treaty, seen by our fathers as shameful, rationally as an historical fact, a generation which did not have to experience the inflation, the world economic crisis and the anarchy of the Germany of the 20's, for us a man like Heinrich will always be an enigma, a fascinating enigma.

Heinrich's friend, and our friend, Werner Roell set himself the task of interpreting this phenomenon of our generation and our time; and of explaining why, almost 50 years after Heinrich's death, people, not only all over Germany, but also in formerly hostile England and America, remember Heinrich with respect and sympathy. With respect for an extraordinary airman and night fighter pilot, with sympathy for a friend and comrade with whom people shared their joys and sorrows, ideals and idols.

We, the young generation of the postwar Germans, must offer our thanks to Werner Roell for the trouble he has taken. We, the family, for whom I may speak here, thank him for the memorial which he was to erect to our uncle through his book *"Laurels for Prinz Wittgenstein"*. But we also owe thanks to all the others who have helped and cooperated to keep Heinrich's memory alive, who have come here today and who, as a token of this memory, have set up this stone here in the grounds of Schönhausen.

The memorial stone at Schönhausen

May this stone also remind future generations of Heinrich Sayn-Wittgenstein the night fighter pilot, of a fascinating and great man and of a proud son of our family."

The last speaker was Werner P. Roell:

'That which moves us today happened almost 50 years ago. In the Second World War, Europe again experienced the horrors of the Thirty Years War. Flourishing cities were reduced to smoking fields of rubble. It is true that the civilian population were supposed to be inviolable, and yet the people experienced untold misery. The suffering was indescribable.

In his sonnet, *"Tears of the Fatherland"*, Andreas Gryphius wrote in 1636:

"But I will not name that
which was worse than death
was harsher than the plague
and fire and starvation
so that spiritual treasures
were wrested from so many."

Since then feelings of hatred, anger and revenge have been overcome. After 50 years we can only mourn. The awful events of the war, this hell on earth are past. They must not be repeated. But we survivors will not forget the brave people who gave their lives. Just recently in London, so today at this memorial stone.

Included in the bravest of the brave are the stretcher bearers who carried the wounded out of the fire, the miner who rescued those who were buried, or the night fighter pilot who defended the homeland. They were all heroes, even if the word "heroism" is, nowadays, oftentimes distorted.

Major Heinrich Prinz zu Sayn-Wittgenstein dedicated himself, life and soul to night fighting. The protection of the defenceless, the women and children, became his burning concern. We honour in him a soldier who fell, and who, renowned by friend and foe was, at the time of his death, the most successful night fighter pilot in the world. With Wittgenstein as *unus pro multis* we remember the men at arms of all the ages whose virtue was bravery and endurance, whose end was sacrifice, and whose legacy was their example. If we did not do this, Goethe's words would fit us:

"A people which parts from its history,
and then finds shame burning its brow,
will be wiped by God from the slate."

Johann Wolfgang von Goethe

Let us leave the soldiers of both sides their honour. The bomber crews too did their damned duty. Let us bow to the dead.

Wittgenstein can speak to us no more. But he left us a legacy: his commitment, his binding example, his chivalry.

As one of millions of German soldiers, and despite growing doubt about the justice of the cause, he fought the hopeless battle until his own death. The memorial stone has been erected so that this soldier, outstanding in his conduct and achievement, this *parfit gentil kyght* will never be forgotten.

I received letters from erstwhile enemies, who are nowadays our allies. We are honoured that they are taking part in this ceremony for one of our bravest soldiers, Prinz Wittgenstein.

Let me quote from a touching letter sent to me by Mr Floyd Williston from Winnipeg in Canada:

"My brother, Flight Sergeant Albert Williston was shot down over Magdeburg on 21 January 1944. I read by chance, in a book about the *Luftwaffe*, that a *Major* Wittgenstein and his radio operator, Sergeant Ostheimer, were in action over Magdeburg that very night and shot down four Lancasters. I have made enquiries about *Major* Wittgenstein and can now better understand the circumstances which persuaded him to fight and die for his Fatherland, and not for the Party.

My brother was equally unswayed by political motives. He fought and died for his country, not because he was anti German, but because he was a patriotic Canadian. He was buried in the Berlin Military Cemetery and I visited his grave. I hope, in the near future, to be able to visit that memorial stone which you are dedicating on 3 October 1992.

It is my firm belief that the events of the last World War should be reported on continuously, so that there can be no repetition of the destruction of the best of the young men our countries brought forth and trained. We should never again be compelled to bear weapons against one another in circumstances beyond our control.

From what I have heard about *Major* Prinz zu Sayn-Wittgenstein, I reckon that, if he were alive today, he would share my conviction."

Wing Commander P B (Laddie) Lucas, CBE, DSO, DFC, a highly decorated fighter commander in the Royal Air Force, wrote in 1983 about Wittgenstein in his 'Wings of War':

"There was a certain young aristocrat who became known during the air battles in the night sky over Germany. He earned considerable respect. Heinrich Prinz zu Sayn-Wittgenstein's story stands way above the ordinary account of experiences."

Now Mr Lucas writes: "I think it is right that after a half century, in which the past pales more and more, that the story of Sayn-Wittgenstein should be told, if only for

'Laddie' Lucas DSO DFC

one reason: it will give following generations an idea of
the unrivalled dedication to flying on both sides - in the
Luftwaffe as well as in the Royal Air Force - in those
frightful years which people call the Second World War.

What few, who did not live in those turbulent times,
can imagine, is the chivalry displayed by those who led the
Geschwader, Gruppen and *Staffeln* of both friend and foe.

The story of Wittgenstein bears witness to this."

So much for two former enemies.

Finally let us remember Wittgenstein again with a
word from Corneille from 'The Ideal Knight':

Werner Roell speaks at Schönhausen

"He pursued his soldierly calling with decency and circumspection and could claim to preserve its humanity. Thus may he find favour in the eyes of God."

The ceremony is over. The hunting horns sound the call, 'The hunt is over'.

CHAPTER ONE

BEGINNINGS AND YOUTH

Who was this *'Major'* Wittgenstein, as he used to call himself and insisted on others calling him? This volume will be about him and his fate, and also show where his life fits into his times and their history.

Heinrich Alexander Ludwig Peter Prinz zu Sayn-Wittgenstein, to give him his full name, was born on 14 August 1916 in Copenhagen (Denmark). He was the second of three sons born to a German diplomat, Gustav Alexander Prinz zu Sayn-Wittgenstein (1880-1953) and his wife, Walpurga, née Freiin (Baroness) von Friesen (1885-1970). In 1919 the father left the Diplomatic Service and the family moved to Switzerland. It is clear that the Wittgensteins felt themselves to be Germans, even if they did live abroad. This was particularly true of Prinz Heinrich, as we shall see later.

What sort of a family did Prinz Heinrich stem from? The Grafen (Counts) von Sayn were first mentioned in documents around the year 1079. The Sayn lands were enjoying increasing prosperity and greater significance which reached an apogee around the year 1250. The Sayn estates soon extended from Koblenz to Köln (Cologne) and from the Dill to the Mosel. In the middle of the 14th Century, Graf Salentin von Sayn married the hereditary Gräfin (Countess) Adelheid von Wittgenstein, a name which probably derives from Wittekind. The Sayn and Wittgenstein estates were amalgamated, the lands on the Lahn and Eder being added.

The now united families produced, in the coming centuries, a series of important personalities. To name but a few:

Граф Витгенштейнъ Генералъ отъ Кавалерiи.
Le Comte de Wittgenstein Général de Cavalerie.

Ludwig Adolf Graf (Count) zu Sayn-Wittgenstein
as a Russian Cavalry General.

One of them was a forebear of the Grafen (Counts) von Sayn. The family chronicles call him an 'outstanding warrior'; he was Graf Heinrich III, named 'The Great'(1202-1246). Amongst other things he took part in the Fifth Crusade. One of the more significant events of his life was a charge of heresy brought against him by the Inquisitor, Konrad von Marburg. But Henricus Magnus cleared himself and was acquitted by Pope Gregory IX. Heinrich caught his enemy when the latter was riding through the Sayn lands and had him killed. That, for the time being, was the end of the Inquisition in Germany.

Another extraordinarily significant personality among the ancestors was Ludwig Adolf Graf von Sayn-Wittgenstein (in Russian Pyotr Khristyanovich Vitgenshtein). He was born in 1769 near Kiev. His father had joined the Russian Army in 1752 and eventually became a Lieutenant General. The son became a soldier at the early age of 12, was a major at 24, and, for bravery, was given early promotion to Lieutenant Colonel. In 1801, as a Major General, he took over command of a Regiment of Hussars, fought against Napoleon at Austerlitz in 1805, and distinguished himself at the battle of Friedland in 1807. As a Lieutenant General, the Czar entrusted him with command of the Hussars of the Life Guard. In 1812, the Wittgenstein Corps, although pressed by the overwhelming strength of the Grande Armée, succeeded in stopping the French advance on St Petersburg. This significant action effectively destroyed the legend of French invincibility in Russian eyes and brought Wittgenstein fame and prestige. He achieved literary fame in 'War and Peace', where Tolstoy referred to him as 'the brilliant hero of St Petersburg'. By way of gratitude, Wittgenstein was presented with an ikon of the Archangel Gabriel with the inscription '*Honorem meum nemini dabo*' (I cede my honour to none). The family arms bear the motto to this day.

In the hard winter campaign on the Beresina, the General forced a French division to capitulate and, by this, made a decisive contribution to the heavy losses suffered in the aggressors' retreat. With strategic far-sightedness, Wittgenstein had two aims in view, the pursuit of the

The Arms of the Wittgenstein family.

enemy and an alliance with Prussia. About Napoleon, he said: 'I will give the Corsican no rest by day, or by night.' And his Quartermaster General, von Diebitsch, met the

Prussian General, Yorck von Wartenburg, who, without his King's approval, agreed to the Convention of Tauroggen.

After the death of Prince Kutuzov, Wittgenstein, still only 44, was appointed Commander in Chief of the Allied Forces. The envy of more senior generals, and views differing from those of his Imperial master, forced him into resignation; he asked to be relieved of his duties. Not until 1813, in the Battle of the Nations at Leipzig, did he take part in the war again with his cavalry. The Wittgenstein Corps went on to ride as far as France. There, however, the Field Marshal was severely wounded. It was true that he was highly decorated and awarded the Order of Saint Andrew, but he was unable to take part in the Paris Victory Parade.

Czar Alexander I appointed Wittgenstein to the Council of State. Alexander's successor, Nicholas 1, promoted him to Field Marshal. In 1834, King Friedrich Wilhelm III and the Czar created him a Prince of both Prussia and Russia. It was said of him that no man was his superior, either in courage or in aggression. In his memoirs Napoleon named Wittgenstein as 'the most able of all Russian generals'.

Wittgenstein's son, Ludwig, latterly an ADC to the Czar, returned to Germany where he re-acquired his family's hereditary seat at Sayn. Endowments settled on Wittgenstein by the Czar were either destroyed or confiscated during the Bolshevik Revolution.

The author considers that a place in this book, dedicated to a soldier, also belongs to an ancestral lady, who was distinguished for her extraordinary beauty. The lady was Leonilla zu Sayn-Wittgenstein, née Princess Baryatinsky. She was born in 1816 and died in 1918 at the age of 102 years. There are three pictures which bear witness to her and her times. In 1837 Horace Vernet painted, in the style of the age, an equestrian portrait of the 21 year old Leonilla Ivanovna Baryatinskaya,

Leonilla Fürstin (Princess) zu Sayn-Wittgenstein.
(Painting by Franz Xaver Winterhalter)

Prinzessin zu Sayn-Wittgenstein. Vernet (1789-1863) was among the great society painters of his time. The picture shows the Princess surrounded by her husband, Prinz Ludwig Adolf Friedrich, the children of his first marriage, Peter and Marie, and her own first son, Friedrich, in the arms of a nurse. The painting is three metres high, over two metres wide, and hangs in the new Pinakothek in München.

Leonilla was the daughter-in-law of the Field Marshal. Contemporaries called her 'one of the most beautiful women of the 19th Century, itself so rich in beauty'. Born into the witty and polyglot society of St Petersburg, she was regarded as conscientious, dutiful and constant. At the age of 18, she married the eldest son of the Field Marshal, Prinz Ludwig zu Sayn-Wittgenstein. Czar Nicholas I, a stern, unartistic man, found no pleasure in the life of St Petersburg society. The francophile Leonilla, as she was called, moved to Paris. The second picture of Leonilla, a lithograph by Franz Xaver Winterhalter, who originated from the Black Forest and was much in demand as a Court painter and portraitist to the high nobility in Paris, dated from this time. The Princess's stay in Paris did not last long, since she was caught up in the confusion of the 1848 Revolution. Terrified, she fled to Berlin where she enthusiastically devoted herself to the Roman Catholic Church. With her friend, the Empress Auguste, she opposed Bismarck, sided with France in 1870/71, and, widowed at the age of 50, went to Switzerland where she lived until her death in 1918. Historically, she represented a whole epoch, outlived the fall of the monarchies in France and Germany, and before her death learned of the Revolution in her Motherland. With her died an age of unchallenged authority, culture and beauty. What have remained are her charitable foundations.

As the last in this series of characters, let us give the word to a scion of the family who brings our thoughts back to the subject of this book, Prinz Heinrich Wittgenstein. The 20 year old Heinrich Stanislaus von Wittgenstein, a cadet in the Bundeswehr, bears not only the name of his great-uncle, but is astonishingly like him in appearance and behaviour. Reserved and yet helpful, he comments on my recollections. He wrote to me in 1991 - very recently:

'What I have been able to learn about my great-uncle makes me very proud and inspires me, as I already feel myself very close to him, because we have the same name. But I also feel committed to emulate his outstanding achievement, but naturally in a more contemporary field.'

He continues:

'It is far from my intention to belittle the military tradition. After completing the Abitur, I enlisted in the Bundeswehr for a two year engagement. However, I hope we are approaching an era in which we shall have banished all weapons of mass destruction. An international peace army, which UN forces already are, should continue to exist. All countries should support such an army with volunteers. This would be a supervised Peace Force which would make it impossible for one nation to arm against another. Its objective should be to prevent the repetition of a World War.'

He closes with the following words:

'It would be presumptuous to demand that I should ensure continuity of achievement. That would be to give praise before the event. However I did not want you to go without my contribution. I should be grateful if you would see the latter as coming under the heading "Upholding Tradition".'

Prinz Heinrich at the age of 10

Let us return to the life of Heinrich Prinz zu Sayn-Wittgenstein. Not very much is known about his early childhood years. They passed peacefully and largely without worries, when one leaves out of account that Heinrich did not enjoy the best of health. Between the ages of 6 and 10, the otherwise normal years of primary schooling, Heinrich initially received private education in Switzerland. In 1926 he was sent to a boarding school at Neubeuren (Upper Bavaria), where he remained until 1932. This phase was interrupted twice: in 1927 for a stay in Davos, occasioned by his health, and in 1929 by a short period at a private school in Montreux. Then in 1932 he was transferred to the Realgymnasium (High School) at Freiburg im Breisgau which he left in 1935 after completing the *Abitur* (Leaving Certificate).

After his arrival in Freiburg, he joined the Hitler Youth, and, by 1935, had become a Group Leader. Following the *Abitur*, he completed his service in the *Reichsarbeitsdienst* (National Labour Service). In 1936 he reported to the 17th Cavalry Regiment in Bamberg. Ten years before him, Claus, Graf Schenk von Stauffenberg, who was later to make an attempt on Hitler's life, became a soldier in the same place. Subsequently the Prinz decided

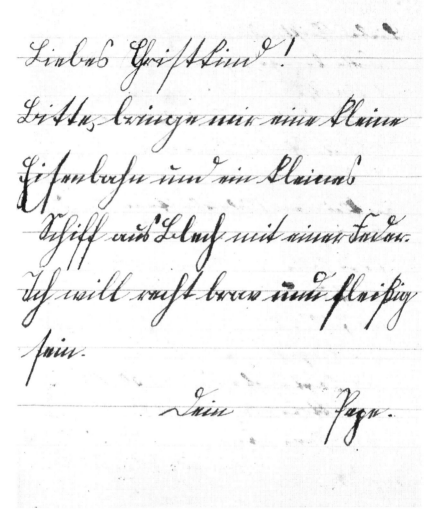

Heinrich wrote this letter when he was seven years old.
The text reads: 'Dear Christchild!
Bring me a small railway and a small ship made of tin and a
pen. Your Pepe.'

Heinrich (right) aged 13 with his older brother Ludwig (left) and his younger brother Alexander.

to join the *Luftwaffe*. In October 1937 he was admitted to the Flying School in Braunschweig (Brunswick), and in June 1938, promoted to *Leutnant*. In *Schlachtgeschwader 40* at Regensburg-Obertraubling, he flew on the Sudeten operation as the author's air-gunner in a Heinkel He 45 armoured biplane. The friendly relationship between us dated from that time. After finishing his flying training, he was stationed at various airfields and flew with several different *Kampfgeschwader*[1]. After the outbreak of World War II, he chalked up 150 operations in Belgium, Russia, France, and against England, with *Kampfgeschwader 1, 'Hindenburg'*.

To return to his youth again. When he entered the boarding school at Neubeuren, he was described as being dark blond with blue eyes, rather unruly hair and slender frame. He was the youngest and, with his delicate health, the weakest at the same time. In spite of this he attracted

[1] *Kampfgeschwader - usually three Gruppen*

Family photo from 1932, Heinrich(right), 16 years old, with his mother and his two brothers.

supporters, even older boys, who would have gone through fire for him. He captivated with his decency and courage. With his strong will he forced himself, despite his poor health, to the toughest achievements, avoided the easy option, did not smoke and enjoyed a versatile training in sports. Later he became an enthusiastic motorcyclist and car driver.

In Freiburg, where he was known simply as 'Heiner Wittgenstein', he was, by contrast with his elder brother, 'the little Prinz'. Recalling a school excursion to the Island of Sylt, a school friend later described him as fun loving, a good comrade who was up to all the tricks and, in the evening, more inclined to go out on expeditions than to bed. He was full of ideas and plans, and flying exercised a great attraction for him even then.

Many letters written by Prinz Heinrich during his boarding school days have survived. Almost without exception, they confirm what a lively, switched on and interested boy he was. Thus he wrote, on 12 February 1928, about his medical stay in Davos:

'Dear Mami! Many thanks for the good chocolate I found in the last laundry basket. We had some very interesting ice-hockey games here last Tuesday, Wednesday and Thursday. On Tuesday Sweden played Davos. Sweden won 4-3. On Wednesday Germany played Warsaw. Warsaw won 8-0. On Thursday, the Swedes again, this time against Germany. The Swedes won 7-0. I watched all those ice-hockey games. It is now fairly cold and snowing pretty heavily. I am just reading Karl May's "In the Land of the Silver Lion". To start with it is about America and then about Arabia, about Hadschi Halef Omar Ben Hadschi Darwud al Gossarah who also plays a big part in "The Slave Caravan". I haven't got any more to tell you for now. Many greetings and kisses.'

Heinrich signs this like all other letters at this time *'Your Pepe'*.

Before Heinrich became an enthusiastic motor-cyclist and car driver he was, in his youth, an equally dedicated cyclist. There is scarcely a letter from that time in which there is not a mention of a bicycle in one context or another. On one occasion he is waiting for the bicycle to be sent back to him after necessary repairs; he asks if he can take his bicycle with him on holiday; he reports on cycle trips, and on a kilometre counter he had bought. But his scholastic achievements were also acceptable. In a letter dated 1928, he wrote that in Latin he rates between 2 and 3, and that in French, he got a 2 for the first exercise and a 1 for the second.

Most of the letters Prinz Heinrich wrote in his youth were concerned with everyday things; he asked for stamps or fare money; he reported regularly on the weather and on his activities in and out of school. Only on one occasion did he worry about something which went beyond the personal. On 31 January 1930, when he was scarcely 14 years old, he wrote to his parents:

> *'Where did you see "All Quiet On The Western Front"? It's supposed to be one of the worst propaganda films ever made. In Germany it was banned on the spot. Remarque did something quite irresponsible, in that he simply wrote about a war in which he was just not involved'.*

As noted, Heinrich wrote this as a 14 year old, three years before the 'seizure of power' by the National Socialists.

What sort of chap was Heinrich, what sort of a character? There is much testimony and documentary evidence on this subject. The most impressive testimony is contributed by his mother. Walburga Prinzessin zu Sayn-Wittgenstein wrote about his youth:

> *'On two occasions we spent the winter months at Oberstdorf in the Allgäu. Heinrich made his first efforts on skis when he was four years old. Even friends noticed how tenaciously and consistently he repeated the same exercise, hour after hour. Some years afterwards I found him covered in snow at the foot of the big ski-jump. A man, standing nearby, was lecturing him: "When you are not even seven years old, you don't take on the big jump." Because he was so light in weight, this jump did not hurt him. It was the start of "living dangerously". Moreover I had plenty of opportunities to live by my principle that a mother of sons must not be anxious.'*

Heinrich had two brothers. The elder, Ludwig, was also killed in the war; the younger, Alexander, had a fatal accident after the war.

On the subject of his early schooling, Princess Walburga reported:

'Since the governesses we at first engaged could, frankly, not cope with him and his brother, who was a year older, we decided to consign the boys to the local village school. Even before they joined the class, the schoolmaster said: "We'll show those dodgy little princeboys what's what". But, after two weeks, the 'dodgy princeboys' had so many allies in the class that they could fight successful battles against the rest. During this period, Heinrich shared the interests of most boys of his age, but, in his case, to a particularly intense degree.'

Princess Walburga then described the young Heinrich's total passion for motor cars:

'Whole exercise books were filled with drawings of the various makes. There were also many of his own design with huge, elegant radiators - always racing cars. The noise of an aircraft at lunch, or at school impelled a rush for the window. There was absolutely nothing you could do about it. When we had to visit a doctor on account of a childhood illness, the doctor said: "The boy must be very difficult. I can see that. But let him grow. Don't try to break his will. It will be alright. He cannot do otherwise than grow good". Subsequently I followed this advice and what else could I have done!'

*Prinz Heinrich drew this dream car
when he was just eleven years old.*

Opposite: a letter from the Prince dated
3 January 1927 the text of which is as follows:

*'Dear Parents. On Monday, Tuesday, Wednesday
and Thursday we had very good skiing here.
Today we can only sledge. When is Uncle Hans
coming here? Udi can get a chain for his lock
here. The Sister said I should not take the
medicines I brought from the hospital because
she does not know when I should take them.
What kind of car is Papa buying this time?
Please send me some more stamps for swaps.
When shall I get the bicycle? Many greetings and
kisses to you both and to Putz. Your Pepe.'*

Heinrich's mother is sure that his understanding of
machines developed at an early age:

Liebe Eltern!

Montag, Dienstag, Mittwoch
und Donnerstag haben wir
hier sehr gut Ski fahren können.
Heute kann man nur noch gut
Schlitten fahren. Wann kommt
Onkel Hans zurück. ?? Übia be?
kommt ??? ??? ??? ??? für
??? Schloß. Die Schwester hat ge-
fragt, daß ich die Medizinen durch
??? ??? ??? ??? ??? ???
haben nicht ??? soll weil ???
??? ??? ??? ??? soll.
??? für ??? ??? ??? ??? ???
??? ??? ??? ??? ??? ???
??? ??? Wann bekomme das
? Rad.
   Viele Grüsse
         und Küsse
             an euch
                und a
                    Putz.
         Euer
              ? Pepe!

'At that time we lived on a steep stretch of country road. As soon as the weather made it at all possible, races were organised on this road with soapboxes, scooters and handcarts, and in winter on sledges, where possible with numbers on their backs, and stopwatches. It was also another opportunity to live dangerously and to overcome fear.'

Walburga continued:

'After Heinrich had, again, just escaped falling under a car, we decided to send the children to a boarding school, but the main reason was that they had got to go to a High School. They were to be educated in Germany and went to Neubeuren near Rosenheim. At the age of 9, Heinrich was by far the youngest and, physically, the weakest. What does a boy do when he is the youngest and the weakest in the class and still wants everything to go his own way? He does exactly the same thing as in the village school and recruits himself a bodyguard.'

Princess Walburga quoted her son:

'You know, Mammi, I go up to a big chap and give him a bit of cheek. He thinks he can do what he likes with me. At this stage, I only need to give a sign, and then the others join in.'

His mother's assessment was as follows:

'Heinrich collected supporters with his uncompromising decency, his comradeship through thick and thin, his physical and moral courage and also his fertile imagination. Time

after time there were boys, sometimes much bigger than Heinrich, who allied themselves with him, not always to the pleasure of the masters and others responsible for his education.'

His mother also recalled:

'When I went to Neubeuren after his first year, the Headmaster had a lot of praiseworthy things to report. "But," he added,"when I order the class to do something, I am often told Heinrich Wittgenstein has forbidden that. I should like to know who issues the orders round here, I or that little fellow." Recently he had thought up something which was particularly cunning. He ordained that it was unfriendly to get less than the lowest mark set as a limit, and this was very low. "But," added the Headmaster,"the boy has positively phenomenal willpower. I have never come across anything like it. If we succeed in pointing him towards a great goal, I shall not have suffered in vain."

Walburga also spoke about her son's delicate health:

'As Heinrish suffered repeatedly from feverish colds, and since I was afraid that the strict regime that he forced on himself would, sooner or later, cause complications with the masters or the mothers of his school friends, we decided to send him to the Friederizianum in Davos, in order to strengthen him physically and cool him off a bit psychologically. He liked it very much in Davos. It is true he went on getting sore throats and the Sister, who had become very fond of him, wrote: "His delicate health is always a source of worry to me".'

But he had particularly stimulating history lessons there and probably the same master taught him German. These aroused a boundless and fervent patriotism in him and the desire to commit himself to his country. He wanted to become a German officer, but he knew how difficult it then was to be accepted by the *Wehrmacht*. From that time onwards, he subordinated his life and behaviour with exclusive single mindedness to this one idea. Now he began to train himself systematically and submitted himself to the strictest discipline. He avoided everything which could undermine his health and, to the end, did not smoke and only drank wine now and again. He was ascetically severe with himself, and was unusually modest in his needs. He found it quite intolerable when somebody asked about his health. 'I hate it,' he wrote to me, 'when people constantly behave as if I were weak and sickly.'

Heinrich's will directed itself elsewhere too:

'He began to save up for a car in a systematic and determined way. Heinrich only went by train when he could not somehow go on foot. He nearly always had a swim where it cost him nothing. He never bought sweets. Everything was put on one side for the car.'

'Subsequently he turned up looking pretty exhausted, having come from Freiburg im Breisgau on his bicycle. "Where did you spend the night?" he was asked, "Somewhere in a wood," was the laconic reply. "What did you have to eat?" "I took a couple of slices of bread with me, and then cherries." He is hardly likely to have bought the cherries at a fruiterers. At all events, he did not spend a single penny on the whole 300 kilometre journey, but saved all the journey money for his car.'

Princess zu Sayn-Wittgenstein wrote:

'In Davos he became much more robust and so returned to Neubeuren, where he remained until 1932. On the very first day in Davos he joined the Hitler Youth, which had just then been banned. As leader of a Hitler Youth group with a number of boys who took part in the group, despite the Swiss ban, he once had to climb out of the window at three o'clock in the morning and hold his training session by moonlight. In order to spare him and ourselves embarrassment and difficulties, we arranged for him to live privately. We knew his absolutely reliable and decent character and were aware that he did not need the discipline of a boarding school. Apart from this, I always approved everything which would make the boys self reliant early in their lives.

His savings had grown to such an extent, that he was able to buy a secondhand lightweight motorcycle. It did not require a driving licence. In the summer holidays, he travelled on his own from Freiburg to the North Sea. It seems to have been a pretty wearing and adventurous trip with cloudbursts and tumbles. We were without news for a long time. I had particularly asked him not to travel in Hitler Youth uniform. Unfortunately, he could not resist the temptation - he had in the meantime become paramilitary sports leader of 113 Group - and things went badly for him. He was shot at from a wood and a bullet penetrated the suitcase strapped on behind him. We did not at all events hear about this, by chance, till one and a half years later.'

Heinrich's mother explained why she was telling this story:

'It feels almost ridiculous to talk about these peacetime dangers and hardships. Nowadays everyone of his age will have had similar experiences, sometimes even worse. It is just meant to show that his youth was filled with consciously sought out difficulties which would help to strengthen him and get him good shape for his future career. "When you want to achieve something, you must always have it in your mind," he often said.'

So much for the memories of a mother about her son. There is testament to Heinrich's behaviour and health which complements that of his mother. The principal of the North Sea School Camp in Wyk on the Island of Föhr wrote to his parents in Switzerland on 19 August 1932:

'Heinrich has been here for 14 days. My judgement of him has not changed. He is difficult to see through because he is quiet and reserved. What strikes one externally is the continuing childlike manner of a boy who is already sixteen years old. He is still all boy, quite uninhibited, and free of all eccentricities. From this I conclude that, on the inside is an uncorrupted human being.'

The letter from the North Sea continued:

'Unfortunately, in spite of the good weather, Heinrich has not yet been able to swim in the sea. He arrived here with a fairly bad attack of bronchitis. I hoped that, with the change of

climate, this would quickly clear up, as is often the case. But the attack was obstinate and has only just begun to recede. In general during these years particular attention will have to be paid to the physical development of this fast growing boy. He is well trained up and tough, but he quite clearly belongs to the asthenic type, has a bad posture and a flat chest. Gymnastics and breathing exercises are bound to have a preventive and corrective effect in this case.'

(Opposite) Prinz Heinrich's School Leaving Certificate.

High School, Freiburg im Breisgau

Leaving Certificate

Heinrich Prinz zu Sayn-Wittgenstein
born on 14 August 1916
at Copenhagen
Lutheran Religion, son of Counsellor of
Legation(Ret) Gustav Alexander Prinz zu S-W
has attended this High School since 13 April 1932 in Form U II and

has been since 24 April 1935 a pupil in the Upper VIth.

He has passed the Leaving Certificate Examination at the School.

General assessment of physical, character and intellectual efforts and overall success: In PT and the scientific subjects, his earlier, and only very poor, effort has considerably improved in the last three months, and he has nurtured good comradeship with his fellow pupils.

Evaluation of individual subjects:

Religion	satisfactory	Chemistry with Mineralogy	
German	good	and Geology	satisfactory
History	good	Biology	good
Geography	good	Drawing	good
Latin	satisfactory	Music	satisfactory
French	satisfactory	PT	good
English	good	Optional	subjects:
Maths	satisfactory	Greek	____
Physics	satisfactory	Italian	____

Freiburg i Br., 17 December 1935

Chairman of the
Examination Board
pp E. Ganter

The Director of the
High School
E. Ganter

48

Realgymnasium Freiburg i. Br.

Reifezeugnis.

Heinrich Prinz zu Sayn-Wittgenstein,

geboren den *14. August* 19*16*

zu *Kopenhagen*

ev. Bekenntnisses, Sohn des *Legationsrats a. D.*
Gustav Alexander Prinz zu S. - W.

hat das Realgymnasium in Freiburg i. Br. seit dem *13. April* 19*32* von Klasse *U II*
an besucht und war seit *24. April* 19*35* Schüler der *Ober*-Prima.

Er hat die an der Anstalt abgehaltene Reifeprüfung bestanden.

Allgemeine Beurteilung des körperlichen, charakterlichen und geistigen Strebens und Gesamterfolges: *In Leibesübungen und in den wissenschaftlichen*
Fächern hat sich sein früher nur sehr mangelhaftes Stre-
ben in den drei letzten Monaten wesentlich gebessert.
Seinen Mitschülern gegenüber hat er gute Kameradschaft gezeigt.

Wertung der Leistungen in den einzelnen Fächern:

Religion	*genügend*	Chemie mit Mineralogie und Geologie	*genügend*
Deutsch	*gut*	Biologie	*gut*
Geschichte	*gut*	Zeichnen	*gut*
Erdkunde	*gut*	Musik	*genügend*
Latein	*genügend*	Leibesübungen	*gut*
Französisch	*genügend*		
Englisch	*gut*	**Wahlfreie Lehrgegenstände:**	
Mathematik	*genügend*	Griechisch	—
Physik	*genügend*	Italienisch	—

Freiburg i. Br., den *17. Dezember* 19*35.*

Der Vorsitzer
der Prüfungsbehörde:

Der Direktor
des Realgymnasiums:

Druckerei und Verlag H. M. Muth, Freiburg i. Br.

49

CHAPTER TWO

FLYING TRAINING

As we know, Prinz Heinrich zu Sayn-Wittengenstein achieved, despite everything, his ambition to become a soldier. He was held in high regard, loved and respected, despite his general reserve. Former *Oberst* and Chartered Engineer Gerhard Baeker describes him thus: 'We got to know him on a course for *Luftwaffe* ski instructors at Kitzbühel in February/March 1939. Heinrich was a modest and reserved officer who carried out his duties with discipline and good will. Superficially, he seemed a bit on the soft side. Accompanied by a mischievous smile, lightly ironic observations could cross his lips, but he was never hurtful. On contemporary questions and problems he rarely expressed an opinion. I had the impression that his attitude was critical but that, in keeping with his nature, he was reserved and inclined to wait and see. Because of his quiet nature he was popular with his fellows.'

Someone who knew Wittgenstein well is Hans Ring. Ring wrote the following two paragraphs in memory of Prinz Wittgenstein which explain, among other things, why Heinrich transferred from bombers to night fighters: 'There he is, a scion of a very old German family, around whom many legends had grown up even during his lifetime. His tall slim figure, vibrating inside and out like a taut bowstring, the narrow face with its high forehead, the nervy hands... Burning patriotism was the driving force of his life and, as a German officer, the boy saw his fulfilment. In this family, with its international connections and, moreover, living abroad, this was not something which was self evident. He was a cavalry officer then a bomber pilot. But he could just not reconcile himself to the bomber arm and was always trying to get into fighters, as

1939 in Regensburg/Obertraubling, members of
Schlachtgruppe 140.
Prinz Wittgenstein (extreme right), the Author (third from top).

a night fighter pilot. In this he saw the realisation of his concept of a soldier in its purest form; not to be a destroyer but a defender.'

Ring continued: 'With immense energy he worked his way up the ladder. A fanatic will forced a body, which was not built for such feats of strength, to obey. An inexorable critic of his own performance, he was never satisfied with what he had achieved. And, just as he was severe with himself, so he demanded the same toughness from those who flew with him. What, in reality, was despair and helplessness at the idea that he was not doing enough to defend his country, was sometimes put down to ambition. We have to envisage Prinz zu Sayn-Wittgenstein, not as a young flyer storming the heavens, but as a man serious and single-minded beyond his years.'

The change from bomber pilot to night fighter is confirmed by his mother: 'He transferred to night fighters

Letter home dated 9th July 1940 - see page opposite for text.

because he realised that dropping bombs was bound to bring untold suffering down on the civilian population.' And he himself admitted to his mother: 'Night fighting is the most difficult, but also the high point of flying.'

Oberst Karl Hülshoff *Geschwaderkommodore* of *Nacht-jagdgeschwader* 2 from 1 November 1941 to 31 December 1942 - Wittgenstein's predecessor - gave impressive descriptions of the Prinz's early period as a trainee pilot. Of course Hülshoff already knew the Prinz and recounted: 'In the winter of 1938/39 Prinz zu Sayn-

Wittgenstein came to *Kampfgeschwader* 54, based at Fritzlar, as *Leutnant* and *Kampfbeobachter[1]* in the *Stabs Staffel*. At that time I was *Technischer Offizier[2]* on the *Geschwaderstab* and saw, in the following months, the effort he put into qualifying for a pilot's licence as soon as possible. I still remember how proud he was when he told me he had flown an Arado 66 without any particular briefing. At that time he was unequalled in his enthusiasm for flying.'

Letter home 9th July 1940:

Dear Parents,

> *'I'm getting on fine and hope to come to Munich in the near future. The war against England will certainly start soon. Hope you are all well and that you (presumably his mother*) are still in Munich.*
> *Hearty greetings, Heinrich.'*

*The 'you' is in the singular, Du. (Translator's note)

Geschwaderkommodore Hülshoff then lost sight of the Prinz for a time. In late autumn 1941 he received a letter from Heinrich: 'He was sitting in the Night Fighter School at Echterdingen (Stuttgart). It was already taking him too long to finish his training and he begged me to ask for him. In the winter the Prinz appeared at *Nachtjagd-Geschwader* 2 as the youngest second-generation night fighter pilot among the old sweats. Indeed it is unlikely that many of the older pilots suspected that the slim, tall

[1] - *Kampfbeobachter - navigator*

[2] - *Technischer Offizier - Technical Officer*

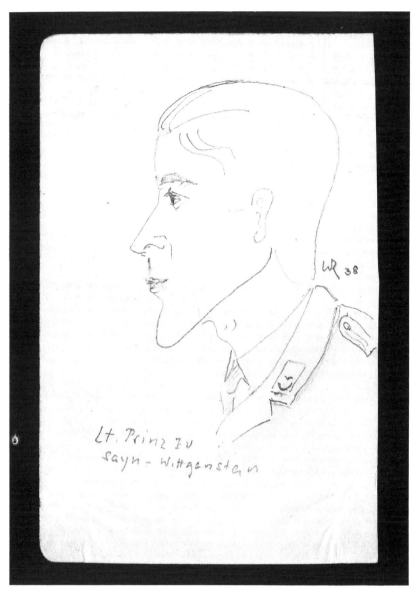

A sketch made by the Author in 1938. Note the initials 'WR'

and mostly brooding Prinz would become a night fighter
pilot who would soon make himself talked about. When we
were chatting he told me that he had more or less got his

54

pilot's licence on a teach-yourself basis, and then, when he heard of the first night fighter successes, put in for a transfer; he was very pleased when the application was granted.'

The following illustration by Hülshoff shows the zeal, in the full sense of the word, with which Prinz Heinrich set about his job: 'In the first few days and weeks after he joined the *Geschwader*, the Prinz took every opportunity to fly with a partner into one of the areas designated *'Hamster', 'Biber'* and *'Zander'*, to practise and improve cooperation with the Fighter Control Officers over and over again. The Fighter Controllers were surprised and impressed by this beginner's seemingly untiring eagerness to learn. Less enthusiastic were members of the ground crew who were hard put to it to keep the Ju 88 serviceable between sorties.'

On home leave. Visiting his Uncle Stanislaus.

'Yes,' Hülshoff continued, 'this thought reminds me of another characteristic in the Prinz's behaviour. It was like this: he found out very quickly that, as a night fighter pilot, you would, without a bit of luck, have to wait quite a long time for a 'kill'. This was particularly so if you were waiting in the *'Hamster'* or *'Stube'* fighter-control areas while thick swarms were flying through *'Zander'*, *'Tiger'* or *'Löwe'*. The next time, you would be sitting in *'Zander'* and all incoming enemy aircraft would go through *'Hamster'* and pass to the South. At this discovery Heinrich brooded a lot, especially when he was not behind the control column. He had to give a bit of help to a night fighter's luck, even if he went a little out of his way in the process. In the evening, when the aircraft were reported to the control tower as serviceable for take off, the Prinz's aircraft was 'unserviceable'. However, as soon as enemy aircraft were identified and the areas they were routed through were crowded, Heinrich's aircraft was suddenly serviceable and he was positively feverish until cleared for take-off. It is true that he had his first successes during this period of ground controlled night operations but his great time came in the era of freelance interception, the so-called *'Zahme Sau'*[3] technique.

Hülshoff went on to give an account of the young officer's first exploits: 'One evening, when the British were first dropping 'window'[4] (strips of silver paper), putting all the radars out of action, and ground control with them, then in addition made low level bombing and machine gun attacks on all the night fighter bases in the area of Holland, he took off amid exploding bombs without any airfield lighting, pitch black, straight across

[3] - *The 'Zahme Sau' (Tame boar) method of night fighting was introduced in 1943, shortly after another freelance technique ('Wilde Sau'- 'Wild Boar'). Both methods were used right up to the end of the war (see also 'Translator's Note').*

[4] - *This particular attack was against Köln (Cologne).*

the airfield. He landed an hour later, quite beside himself with rage because his guns had jammed and, for this reason, had 'only' shot down two aircraft. This was his first 'double', which without the jamming would have been even bigger.'

The *Geschwaderkommodore* stressed that Henrich Wittgenstein's performance should be rated highly because, at the time, he was a young, inexperienced night fighter pilot. It was, however, also the beginning of the development of a fighter who, at that time at least, was unusual but who even today, taking into account personal and general circumstances, should not be despised. 'He was a 'young sweat' with his first, beginner's, success, but because of his dare-devil take-off and the two 'kills', without any guidance from ground control, everyone was talking about the Prinz and went on doing so. If he managed to infiltrate the bomber stream, he would hang in there. More than once he shot down five four-engined bombers; more than once fragments of the bomber he was shooting at hit the fuselage or wings of his own aircraft, and more than once, when landing after the fifth 'kill', he would curse problems with the guns. Among the many other distinguished and successful night fighters he made it to the very top'.

It did not belittle the significance of the Prinz when Hülshoff added: 'While fully recognizing his own merits and greatness, I think it fitting, at this point, to remember his crew. It is known that his flight engineer had 'cat's eyes', and it is said that, brought to within 100 metres by the wireless operator, he could identify an aircraft in the prevailing light and, if they were flying in the bomber stream, could often put a choice of several targets in his Prinz's sights. Prinz Wittgenstein knew this very well and very often expressed appreciation of his crew. His gratitude was expressed with reserve and he kept his distance but, for all that, it was no less warm and no less significant. On the day before he was killed he had invited his crew to dinner.

Wittgenstein with his crew.

CHAPTER THREE

THE WAR OF THE BOMBERS

How should one now regard those times and circumstances in which millions of people were placed, whether they wished or not? What was it like in the years from 1939 to 1944, between the beginning of the war and the year in which Prinz Wittgenstein died? It cannot fall to these recollections to investigate the question of war guilt, or to examine and compare all the crimes connected with it. The purpose of this book is simply and solely to describe the life and death of a young German officer. However in this particular case the task is impossible without linking it to those times, particularly the area of life relevant to Wittgenstein; and this was a kind of war not experienced up to this point, a war against the civilian population.

Even today people are convinced that Hitler introduced murderous change into events when he ordered the bombing of the British city, Coventry, and later threatened to wipe out further towns and cities. It certainly is a historical truth that the object of the attack on the industrial city in Central England was to destroy its capacity for producing armaments. Records of the operational briefings for the Coventry raid are still available to be read today. They make the object absolutely clear. At all events, it is also true that casualties among the civilian population could not be avoided and had to be accepted. In the first two years of the war the German Luftwaffe was still strong enough to deal out such blows.

Only in 1942/43 did the tide turn. The Allies, in particular the British, had decided to use carpet bombing to destroy the supposed will to resist of the German population. This is not the place to explain why this assessment was false or how the Allied leadership could conceive the idea of waging such a murderous war. It is established that from a certain time in 1943 onwards, in the Western part of Germany, not a night passed when the population did not have to go down to the air raid shelter. For months, and often for years, women and children spent their nights in the primitively furnished shelters. The more the Americans got involved in the war, and the more time passed, the more often it happened that many daylight hours also had to be spent living in the gloom of the cellars.

However, right till the end of the war, the British were responsible for the majority of attacks and they were, macabre but true, 'answerable' for the night. For this reason night fighting, for which Prinz Wittgenstein opted, had a particular significance. This was no war of aggression but air defence, and not only of armament centres alone but, above all, of the civilian population. It was in the latter that Prince Wittgenstein saw his main responsibility. The battle against the incoming bomber streams was fought hard and relentlessly, but fairly.

This chivalry is expressed in mutual respect. Meetings between former enemies from the Royal Air Force were, just a few years after the war, events which outsiders did not begin to understand. So many of the British have given their testimony on the subject of the airman, Heinrich Prinz zu Sayn-Wittgenstein. One of these is Wing Commander P.B. 'Laddie' Lucas, a highly decorated fighter commander of the Royal Air Force. He led a Mosquito unit and made eight 'kills'. As an officer of the Reserve, he calls himself a 'wartime amateur'. A journalist by profession, he became an entrepreneur and a Conservative M.P. in the Lower House of the British Parliament. He wrote a series of books about the Second World War, including 'Flying Colours', the biography of Douglas Bader, a successful fighter pilot despite having lost both legs.

In 1983 Lucas wrote about Wittgenstein in 'Wings of War': 'There was a successful young German aristocrat who left a lasting impression across the sky of Germany, Occupied Europe and the Eastern Front. He died having earned general public respect. Heinrich Prinz zu Sayn-Wittgenstein's story soars above the normal run of events.'

Now Mr Lucas has written to the author of this book: 'When I wrote those words in 1983, I did not yet know that you were going to write a biography of that remarkable young German officer of noble lineage. I was pleased when I heard that, because I think it right and proper that after a half century, in which the past becomes increasingly dim, the story of Sayn-Wittgenstein should be told. And if only for one reason: it will acquaint future generations with the exemplary commitment to flying on both sides - in the Luftwaffe, as well as the Royal Air Force - in those awful years called the Second World War.'

Lucas continued: 'What few of those, who did not live through those turbulent times, will believe is the chivalry exemplified by those who led the *Geschwader, Gruppen* and *Staffeln* of friend and foe alike. The story of Wittgenstein is a testimony to the chivalrous battle fought by us as opponents in the sky.'

Lucas then goes on to describe his experiences with young airmen of the *Bundesluftwaffe* in our times: 'I have had many opportunities in Germany to talk about my wartime experiences. One evening, after one of my lectures, a young *Leutnant*, a pilot, with impeccable manners and fluent English came up to me saying, "Sir, may I ask you a question?" "Of course," I replied, "I hope I can answer it." "You have talked about your *Luftwaffe* friends, *Generalleutnant* Galland, *Oberst* Neumann, *Oberst* Falck and others. How can they be your friends when you fought against them for years? That is difficult to understand." I tried as best I could to explain. Flyers are a brotherhood, and war the common factor. Then I added:

"When you look back today the whole thing looks like a hard game, in which both sides gave it their all. Now that's a long time ago. The teams meet, sit down harmoniously round a table and talk about their experiences. The game is over." The young *Leutnant* listened attentively, completely absorbed. He paused a little before he commented. "If it is like that, then I think... what shall I say... it was... bloody marvellous." I believe that part of this thought would also apply to Sayn-Wittgenstein. Read history, Werner! I believe you will agree with me.'

CHAPTER FOUR

FIGHTER PILOT

The skill at arms of the fighter pilot is tough, realistic and merciless. The South African, 'Sailor' Malan, one of the most successful pilots on the British side, an instructor and tactician says, among his homilies: 'When you are on the attack, fire only in short bursts of one or two seconds. In the process, think of nothing else. Brace the full weight of your body on the rudder pedals and grip the control column with both hands. Keep your eyes up when turning in to the attack, and particularly when you break away. Don't go on looking at the enemy you have just hit. This is the critical phase. Many are shot down just at this point (presumably this cost Wittgenstein his life). Do not fly straight or at the same height for more than 30 seconds. Go in fast, hit hard and break off the fight carefully.'

The fighter pilot is judged by his score of 'kills'. Looking back in peacetime, it sounds macabre when two top class night fighter pilots, like Wittgenstein and Lent, competing with one another for the victor's laurels, should number off their 'kills' and strive to out-trump each other, as if they were hanging scalps on their belt. This game with death seems brutal and unprincipled. Let us forgive them for using victories in the air as a yardstick, the ambition to be the best in the daily duel with the enemy. They did it without hatred, rather with bitter respect for their opponent, who, like them, was putting his life on the line. Let us forgive them for using sporting competition to shake off the horror and avoid becoming weak.

Is such a book about Wittgenstein altogether appropriate, or even necessary today? A question which is difficult to answer. Walter Wäninger, *Oberstleutnant* (Retd), who used to be a Department Head in the *Bundeswehr* Documentation Centre wrote to the author: 'Wittgenstein said that there were many soldiers who, in the mud and slime, made more sacrifices than he did. He mentioned his brother in this context. It is a good thing that in our day and age, when the only efforts which count are those which are made for personal advantage, that people, especially the young, have this pointed out to them. The latter do not know the lack of freedom in those days, which - out of ignorance of other lifestyles - was not recognized by us boys as being a lack of freedom.'

Wäninger continued: 'We young soldiers were often fearful, but we never had a feeling of guilt. Everything must be judged by the norms valid at the time in question. Nowadays it is just as easy as it is wrong to ask "Why did you...?" The young people of the present day are no cleverer; they live in a different time with different politics, education and society. The spiritual horizon has become much wider. And that is gratifying. Unfortunately egoism, read "self realisation", has grown in step with prosperity. Fatherland is a vague concept. *Volksverbundenheit[1]*, as a relict of the Nazi era, is obsolete.

Wäninger closed his letter to the author with the following thoughts: 'But all periods of time are subject to change. The son of the present day reader will read the book differently from his father. But both retain, possibly even unconsciously, respect for selfless commitment. In

[1] *Volksverbundenheit - community spirit.*

this case, you have saved a courageous German soldier from being forgotten. His commitment, as a high achievement of personality, is unchallenged. You give the reader freedom to make up his own mind. And that is the right thing. I share your conviction that the *Bundeswehr*[2] should be rooted in the tradition of its predecessors '.

[2] - *Bundeswehr - Modern day German armed services.*

CHAPTER FIVE

NIGHT FIGHTING

Before continuing the account of Prinz Wittgenstein's life and death, we need to slot in a more technical chapter which deals with the possibilities of night fighting, commensurate with the state of developments at that time. Even the reader who is less interested technically should not skip this chapter, since it has been so written as to be intelligible to the layman and will clarify descriptions of night fighting. The author is Dr Eng Herbert Kümmritz. During the war he was a *Feldwebel* and Wittgenstein's wireless operator and was involved in 43 'kills'. Wittgenstein helped him to obtain leave for further education in 1943. Kümmritz wrote:

'The range of night vision, considerably reduced in relation to day vision and further circumscribed by clouds and mist etc., presented the night fighters with special and specific problems from the day of their inception. The tactics and practice of night fighting proved to be well nigh impossible without support from the ground. Even help from searchlights to identify enemy aircraft - usually bombers - hardly changed the situation. Partial successes in so-called illuminated (searchlight) night fighting, frequently brought about more by chance than by design, did not alter the fact that a general solution of the night fighting problem had hardly come any closer. By itself the possibility the enemy had, to exploit banks and layers of cloud to conceal their aircraft and direction, made the defenders' problems understandable. Bad weather operations, increasingly favoured by the British as the air war progressed, would have given the German defence system, as it then was, no chance of success.

What was missing was the improvement of the all-

Wittgenstein's radio operator Herbert Kümmritz who was with him during 43 'kills'

weather vision of the fighter, including the concomitant pin-pointing of the enemy. With an average night visibility of 100 metres or, in the most favourable circumstances, 300 metres, a system had to be found which permitted the acquisition of the target enemy aircraft at a range of kilometres. It is true that the obvious solution - if only for short and middle ranges - was the employment of infra-red (in those days it was referred to as ultra-red) radiation. However the technical realities of the 40's made it impossible to use the "active" system (illumination of the target with infra-red searchlights), or the "passive" system (reception of infra-red radiation from the target). A series of trials with specially developed equipment ("Spanner", Kiel Z) were, to the disappointment of the German night fighters, not very promising. It seemed then, by contrast with the present level of technology, to be almost pointless to install the equipment.

The exploitation of another form of electro-magnetic radiation then brought a solution. It was developed and installed more or less simultaneously by both belligerents. The magic word was radio measuring technology or

Dr Eng H. Kümmritz today.

radar[1]. As is well known, this system, now in service on a world wide basis and quite indispensable, exploits the reflection of objects "illuminated" by a high frequency to locate them in three-dimensional space. The position of the antenna directed at the target supplies the elevation and the azimuth (the angle between a direction of reference - as a rule North - and the direction of a line leading to the target). The elapsed time taken by the electro-magnetic waves to reach the target and return gives the range. At this point one has to make a distinction between ground based and airborne equipment. While the known location of the ground based equipment permits the location of the airborne target in terrestrial coordinates (and also does the same nowadays), airborne equipments give the position of the target relative to one's own position. At all events the airborne equipment could also give an absolute measurement of the target's range. The reading - in the form of an impulse - was shown on a two or three tube monitor.

From a chronological point of view, it was the ground stations (*"Freya"* or *"Würzburg"*) which were the first to be taken into service. They were also the first to be

---

[1] *Radar - acronym for radio detecting and ranging.*

enlisted in support of night fighter operations. Irrespective of the state of visibility and weather conditions they successfully determined the position, course and altitude of incoming aircraft. When the figures so obtained were given to our fighters on R/T, they could, henceforth only "half blind", use the constantly corrected information to home in on the enemy. As this also required a continuing and precise definition of our aircraft's own position (not possible at that time), the process was elegantly modified by the addition of a second radar. The *"Himmelbett"*[2] was created for the "dark" night fighters (*"Dunaja"*).

After more or less unsuccessful trials in the years 1942/43 with "light", "dark" or "combined" night fighting techniques, the "dark" version, supported by radar, gradually established itself in the form of the *"Himmelbett* technique"*. The basis for this was the so-called *"Kammhuber Line"*, a strip of territory which ran roughly from Denmark along the Western frontier of Germany to France. The strip was divided into night fighting sectors, which were hemispherical in shape with a radius of 50 - 70 kilometres and which reached an altitude corresponding to the range of the radar equipment employed. At the centre of each sector were two *"Würzburg"* radars and a *"Freya"* (for long distance general search), a radio beacon and an R/T station for communications. The basic idea was that one *"Würzburg"* would cover our own aircraft, and the second, the enemy. Both aircraft were represented on a special map and the night fighter was directed by ground control on to "his" target aircraft by R/T. As a rule this was done via VHF voice broadcast by the Fighter Control Officer (FCO). To display the current plot, a special table was developed, the so-called *"Seeburg"* table, which enabled the locations signalled by the radars to be

---

[2] - *Himmelbett - four poster bed. Dunaja - abbreviation for 'Dunkle Nachtjagd'. Both code words for parts of the nightfighter ops.*

represented on a horizontal table in the form of points of light. "Data transmission" from the radars to the light point projector was dead simple - by word of mouth. It was only later that a machine was invented for this purpose. The FCO's art was to bring the two points of light (blue/red = friend/foe) together, as quickly as possible, by deft direction i.e. by leading our aircraft to the enemy via the shortest route.

The accuracy of this system was by today's standards insufficient; it was of an order of magnitude of plus/minus 300 metres, which meant that, in this (final) phase of the approach, visual contact was not always made. Many an enemy aircraft was able to go on its way without hindrance, although the fighter was only 200 metres away from it. Added to this, the *"Würzburg"* crews were often unpractised and this led to strident complaints from the night fighters. This was particularly true of radar stations deep in German territory.

This weakness was not remedied until *"Lichtenstein"* airborne radars came into service from mid 1942. The radar operated on a wavelength of 60 centimetres and enabled an enemy aircraft to be located at about four to four and a half kilometres. The target came up as an impulse on a cathode ray tube. The fighter's radio operator worked the radar and passed instructions to his pilot on the basis of the data received. This radar achieved much better accuracy, down to plus/minus 150 metres. If the target did not take refuge in cloud he was almost always within visual range of the fighter. The result was in all probability a "kill" (a so-called '*Lichtenstein* kill').

The night fighter's attack was preceded by so-called "course harmonisation", that is to say the fighter flew on the same course, and at the same speed, as the target, and about 50 to 150 metres below. The attack then continued by bringing up the nose of the fighter slightly and firing at the target. The result was that the enemy machine had to fly through bursts from the fighter's horizontally aligned weapons.

This form of attack proved to have a dangerous disadvantage which often led to the fighter's being shot down, since it came almost automatically within range of the bomber's rear gunner. If his aircraft was not already in a dive, the rear gunner could achieve a devastating effect with his quadruple machine guns. Many German night fighter crews paid with their lives for such an attack.

It was clear that thought was given to remedying this situation and a variety of possibilities were kicked around. About 1943 something new had been constructed, which, like many other things, was immediately given a nickname by the troops, the so-called *"Schräge Musik"*. The principle was comparatively simple. Vertically aligned guns were mounted on the upper surface of the aircraft in addition to the horizontal weapons. The vertical guns were adjusted to slant slightly (i.e. *schräg*) towards the nose, hence the *"Schräge Musik"*. This gave the advantage of being able, when in a position reached by course and speed harmonisation - directly underneath the enemy aircraft - to fire in an upward direction. This had several advantages: firstly the fighter was no longer within range of the quadruple guns in the tail; secondly it exploited the bomber's blind spot, where it had no view of the ground. Usually the bombers had no defensive weapons directly underneath. The dangerous aspect of this method was the possibility of being dragged down by the falling bomber. The art of the fighter pilot lay in hitting the bomber full in the underside and then manoeuvring himself smartly away from the area where the bomber would go into a dive. There was a further danger that the fighter's guns would hit the bomb load; in particular when the bomber was carrying parachute mines, there would be an explosion which inevitably destroyed the fighter as well. In this case too, the trick was to hit the enemy without being hit by the fragments from the explosion.

The *"Himmelbett"* technique, linked with the name of

General Kammhuber (later *Inspekteur der Luftwaffe*), lost part of its effectiveness when the enemy gave up flying singly, or in waves, and went over to large formations, the so-called bomber stream. As one can easily imagine from what has already been described, the control system based on the *Würzburg* radars was soon "choked up" by the large number of incoming aircraft. In the end the system was only capable of achieving a small number of interceptions while the enemy bombers were flying through. Even if one occupied a limited area with several fighters and put them in turn and according to circumstances into the bomber stream, only partial successes would be achieved. An improvement to the system was badly needed. It was hoped to achieve greater successes by extending the night fighting sectors further into Germany. This extension was based on the assumption that the bomber streams would penitrate further, as they in fact did from mid 1943 onwards. While the basic idea behind the *"Himmelbett"* technique aimed at the defence of the country on its borders and in a broad belt running from Scandinavia down to France, the available positions had to be stretched to the centre of the country. This was a scheme which highlighted the limitations on home defence and on its possibilities. Even if one assumed that the numbers of fighters available were sufficient it was difficult to set up the many new *"Himmelbett"* stations required; supplying the personnel to man them also caused problems. At any rate, the extension of the sectors resulted in the enemy having to reckon with losses of five to eight per cent for every operation. In the pursuit form of night fighting (*"Zahme Sau"*) deep into Germany the quota of losses rose to 10%.

On both sides new techniques and variants of air warfare were being developed all the time. Thus the British went over to unexpected jamming measures and put them into operation from mid 1943. These measures were used for the first time in the famous/infamous attack on

Hamburg, which went on over a period of several days. The *Kammhuber Line* was virtually condemned to ineffectiveness. The rigidity and complexity of the German night fighting organisation was a victim of fertile British imagination and the flexibility which went with it. An excellently prepared programme of jamming measures made the German radar system virtually ineffective, beginning with the raid on Hamburg in July 1943. Both fixed and mobile jamming stations and, above all, *"Düppel"³* formed part of the British programme. These were dropped from aircraft by the million and were popularly known as *"Lametta"* (tinsel). The people, who had become nervous at the bombing, did not know what to make of the strips at first. To begin with it was thought that they were either poisoned or irradiated, until they turned out to be harmless. They were even collected by children. As long as these harmless looking things danced around in the air they were extraordinarily unpleasant in their effect because they put defensive radar out of action. This was because the strips, on account of their reflective qualities, created the illusion of thousands of targets which were not there at all! German airborne and ground based radars were effectively saturated by the "Window". This was achieved with particular ease against the *"Würzburg"* and *"Lichtenstein"*, both of which operated on the 50 centimetre wavelength. As even navigational aids such as radio beacons and ground based D/F equipment were not immune to jamming, German air defence was, to all intents and purposes, virtually crippled. From the British point of view it was electronic counter measures (ECM or, in German "Eloka"⁴) to perfection; from the German point of

---

³ - *Düppel - 'Window' was the code-name for strips of reflective aluminium foil, cut in strips to a length corresponding to half the radar wavelengths.*

⁴ - *'Eloka' - **Elektronische Kampfmassnahmen***

view it was a catastrophe.

What to do? The only chance clearly lay in concentrating on those forces who had always demanded "freelance" night fighting, that is a method which was not tied to (electronic) equipment. In this context the name to be singled out is that of the then *Major* and bomber pilot, Hajo Herrmann. Together with Lossberg, he pushed through night fighting techniques which have become known under designations such as *"Wilde Sau"* (Wild Boar), *"Zahme Sau"* (Tame Boar) and *"Verfolgungs-nachtjagd"* (Persuit night fighting) etc. Basically these were all variations or special forms of freelance night fighting. Single engined fighters (Me 109's & FW 190's) were usually called upon to defend targets, mostly to protect large towns (*"Wilde Sau"*). The *"Schwere Nachtjagd"* (heavy night fighters - Ju 88's & Me 110's) - (Wittgenstein) - were filtered into the bomber stream and, by *"mitschwimmend"* (swimming with the stream), aimed to shoot down as many enemy aircraft as possible (*"Zahme Sau"*) or (*"Verfolgungsnachtjagd"*). The killing ground was the whole of Germany and the occupied territories. Seen as a whole, these tactics inflicted considerable losses on the enemy. Five to ten per cent of the incoming bombers did not return home. It is true that the losses also resulted from the constantly deepening penetration of Germany by the bombers, which raided cities like Berlin, Leipzig and Munich. On the other hand, the toll in lives which the German fighters had to pay was also considerable. In particular young inexperienced crews often survived only a few operations. This hit the pilots of the single engined fighters, who, in addition to fighting, had to contend with navigational difficulties as well, particularly hard, and in many cases they had to bale out after losing their bearings. Doubts about the real value of *"Zahme Sau"* have been entertained to this day by those with experience and, in the last analysis, the ratio of our losses to those of the enemy was unbearably high.

The so-called *"Schwere Nachtjagd"* (heavy night fighters) were better equipped for the battle by night. They navigated independently, but had to contend with difficulties imposed, partly by the enemy and partly by the weather. By contrast with the early years of the war, when the British bombers only flew in on moonlight nights, they later flew only in bad, cloudy weather. As a result the night fighters were obliged to transfer their activities to bad weather areas, partly above and partly in the clouds. Frequently this happened above the towns under attack, and in cooperation with the Flak[5], who were ordered to avoid firing above certain heights, by using time fuses, yet often fired higher. In this situation, there was often a chance to use the so-called *"Leichentuch"* (shroud). This macabre designation referred to a continuous layer of cloud which, illuminated on the underside by fires and searchlights, made an ideal background to show up the dark British bombers. Despite the Flak's often shooting too high, the bombers thus thrown into relief were attacked by the night fighters and often shot down over the burning town.

Far greater difficulties than those caused by weather conditions arose from tackling the flexibility and technological imagination of the British enemy. If he had, hitherto, already used jamming methods on the grand scale to bring the *"Himmelbett"* system to grief, from the autumn of 1943 he busied himself with the disruption, as far as possible, of the freelance tactics of the German night fighters. This involved continued disruption of the early warning radars by *"Mandrel"* jammers which increasingly affected the air raid reporting broadcasts. The new phase now involved large scale deception air attacks which were easily achieved with the help of the "window" technique

[5] - *Flak (anti-aircraft [ack-ack] defences) German abbreviation of Fliegerabwehrkanone.*

and gave rise to considerably increased night fighter operations which, however, were led astray. In both areas of deception, and greatly to the chagrin of the night fighters, the fast flying Mosquito bomber particularly distinguished itself.

The Mosquito was a multi-purpose wooden aircraft, the strength of which lay principally in its high speed. Even with a bomb load, often a parachute mine, it reached a cruising speed of about 540 k.p.h. At this rate, it was fast enough to outfly practically every German fighter. Only single engined fighters and the only thoroughbred German night fighter, the He 219, could vie with the Mosquito for speed. The German high speed fighter, Ta 154, conceived as an "anti-Mosquito" aircraft, never got beyond the planning stage.

In this context it should be pointed out that, with the exception of the He 219, the aircraft available to the night fighters were not specifically designed for night fighting. There were modified bombers (Ju 88, Do 17, Do 217), and the Bf 110, originally designated as a *"Zerstörer"* (destroyer). They had qualities suitable for night fighting, but were not specifically designed for this purpose. The He 219 came into service in the middle of 1943, albeit in limited numbers, but during the introductory phase suffered from a series of teething troubles. From the time of its conception the He 219 was a really excellent night fighter, but an in-service number of 50 was never exceeded.

In electronic terms, a ding-dong battle was fought on both the British and the German sides. Every piece of new equipment, every new idea promptly evoked an immediate response. On the German side at all events it was more a question of reactions than actions. Apart from the classic applications of high frequencies, a new type of airborne all-round radar brought about the step into centimetre wave technology, hitherto neglected on the German side. The set worked on a 9 centimetre wavelength and was designated the H2S (Home Sweet Home). The Germans dubbed it the *"Rotterdamgerät"* set after the place where it was first found, in a crashed British aircraft near Rotterdam. Because of its short wavelength the set was able to project an image of the countryside it was crossing, rather like a map, on a visual monitor screen. It was excellent for target finding and acquisition and, for this reason, was installed in British "Pathfinder" aircraft. These flew ahead of the main bomber forces, identified the target area with the aid of the "Rotterdam" radar, and then marked it with cascades of flares which slowly fell to the ground. The general public knew them as *"Christbäume"* (Christmas trees), and when they appeared they not infrequently gave rise to a horrified panic, because people knew that bombs would follow the *"Christbäume"*, since the main British bomber force had to drop its bombs within the marked area.

The irony of history lay moreover in the fact that the technique of the "Pathfinders", now employed so successfully by the British, was developed and tested by the Germans during the "Blitz" on Britain.

Obviously the German night fighters strove to shoot down the "Pathfinder" aircraft before they reached the target area. From 1944 a radar listening receiver called *"Naxos"* was very helpful in this regard because it could "D/F"[6] the "Rotterdam" equipment and, with it, the "Pathfinder" aircraft itself. However, given that this radar listening receiver could only measure the bearing, but neither altitude nor range, successes lagged behind expectations. In addition to that, the "Pathfinders" were at the front of bomber formations, which could not always be identified, and were very fast, particularly if they were Mosquitos or fast Lancasters. This meant that, so far as *"Schwere Nachtjagd"* were concerned, they were practically impossible to catch.

[6] - *D/F - Direction finding.*

In this connection it is perhaps interesting that on the German side there was also a switch to deception methods after the "Rotterdam" set had proved itself to be virtually unjammable. The deception was based on triple mirrors. These were metallic reflectors which, as vertical sheets of metal on floats in lakes and rivers, but which were also set up on land, gave the false impression of non-existent targets.

In the electronic warfare between attack and defence, night fighter warning systems assumed a certain significance on the British side. There were two different kinds, one was passive, the other active. "Passive" in this case meant the British were able to pick up radiation from a German radar and evaluate it; this was particularly so in the case of the German *"Lichtenstein"* airborne radar. The only counter measure was to switch off the *"Lichtenstein"* when the enemy had been identified visually. The "active" method consisted of radars which transmitted astern and were intended to give warning of approaching German night fighters. This system had an obvious boomerang effect, since the German fighters concerned were now able to locate the target enemy through its own radar. The *"Flensburg"* radar used for this purpose was also suitable for "D/F-ing" and locating enemy ground based jamming stations.

In the totality of events, British jamming operations remained decisive. *"Würzburg"* and *"Freya"* were, it is true, later redeveloped as broad band radars and this made it possible to switch to alternative frequencies. However, because of the wobbling of the jamming frequencies, these radars could not be completely immune to jamming. A further counter measure employed made it possible, by exploiting the Doppler effect, to distinguish between moving targets and those which were virtually stationary, or slowly drifting. An additional switch in the *"Würzburg"* *("Würz-Laus")* ensured that moving targets (bombers) appeared on the screen as wandering dots, in contrast to the reflections arising from "window"; they wandered over the screen like a louse. A similar technique was used on the considerably slower *"Freya"* equipment.

With airborne equipment other ways were used. By a clear reduction of the working frequency - increasing the wavelength to several metres - and making it possible to switch in scatter waves (2.5-8 metres), notlceable improvements in the *"Lichtenstein SN 2"* were achieved, particularly against "window".

Similarly, British jamming activities against ground to air communications caused great problems in night operations. The plain language R/T messages broadcast by German fighter control centres were either distorted to the point of being unintelligible, or counterfeited, the latter being frustrated by the introduction of morse code. After boosting the output of German transmitters, inter alia by using national broadcasting stations, the British went over to broadcasting false reports on the same wavelength. Naturally this caused considerable confusion among the night fighter crews. Musical messages were the answer from the German side. These indicated which towns were under attack. Deception was also practised in this field. The introduction of women's voices brought some success, because the British shrank from letting women fly in deception aircraft.

In spite of everything, the success of the German night fighters was considerable up to the summer of 1944. Every operation into Germany cost the British five to ten per cent losses. Ten per cent was the critical level for Bomber Command. However, in this context it must be remembered that the British squadrons were continually increasing the depth of their penetration and their exposure to danger was protracted. This fact, coupled with the much less dangerous daytime penetrations by US formations, caused Bomber Command to reach a decision that their night operations, in the then current form, should be moderated. Alongside occasional heavy bomber incursions, they increasingly went over to disruptive attacks flown by Mosquitos. At first there were only a few, but their numbers soon increased to average 40 to 60. They dropped relatively unaimed parachute mines and beyond that they were able, by flying in on a broad front, to stir up the whole of Germany. Because of both their high speed and service ceiling (10,000 metres) the German defence could scarcely reach them. On the German side, this situation reawoke the long since abandoned idea of fighting the Mosquitos with the jet fighters, just then being brought into service, the Me 262 and Ar 234 (also for night flying). Apart from individual successes, circumstances early in 1945 prevented a larger commitment of these aircraft types. Only the two-seater Me 262 with electronic equipment could be made available to the squadrons in small numbers.'

Kümmritz concludes his report on the technology of German night fighting with the following sentences: 'The German night fighters, even if they, apart from the long range night fighting over the UK broken off in 1942, and by reason of prevailing circumstances, could not act but only react, nevertheless displayed courage and high morale right up to the last days of the Second World War. Just a few days before the end of the war, top grade crews were able to report large numbers of "kills". Altogether the German night fighters shot down close on 8,000 enemy aircraft.'

There are, naturally, other, less technical accounts of night fighting. We owe one of them to one of the war reporters who resisted the temptation to subordinate himself to the propaganda machine of the Third Reich. One of these war correspondents was Jürgen Clausen, who got to know Wittgenstein on operations, and who was killed on the night of 19/20 February 1944 with his pilot *Hauptmann* Peters on a night operation against British bombers. He survived Wittgenstein by only a month. *Hauptmann* Erhard Peters (23 kills) and his crew are not forgotten. Mercifully free of pathos and propaganda, Clausen wrote seriously and humorously, in soldiers' language, a long and gripping account of night fighting from which the following lengthy excerpts are taken.

Clausen wrote: "I have now been with the night fighters for over three months and everything is quite different from what I had imagined. Or, to put it more accurately, the accents have been transposed. Just as one can see, when going through a number of different graphological assessments of the same person, that while all the experts have more or less noted the same groups of characteristics, every one of them will have felt that quite different personal qualities were dominant, primary and especially significant.

Naturally, I had formed a picture of night fighting in advance and, for sure, heard or read a lot of things about it which were true. At all events, this imaginary picture gleamed in a rather adventurous, uncertain light, rather like the monstrous turbulent sky in El Greco's magnificent picture of Toledo. One always feels an indefinable kind of inner excitement when one comes to a new arm of service. Time and again, one is tempted at first to make typological observations and to ascribe typical characteristic to the individual arms of service. I saw our crews for the first time at a met. briefing. They stood in a half circle in front of the excellent meteorologist, who, in an assumedly melancholy civilian life as a senior master, had taught boys of the Lower Sixth Form in Vienna. He liked very much to herald the imminent conclusion of his briefing with the mysterious humanistic phrase "Ergo, of which..." This became a standard quotation.'

Clausen's description of the air crews and their customs is very amusing: 'To start with, I could not distinguish who was actually the pilot, who the wireless operator and who the air gunner. They were all garbed in the same thick clothing: in black fur boots, tastefully lined in white, and quite enormous trousers. On my own trousers I later counted seven zip fasteners and at least five large pockets. But they are a kind of magic trousers. You never rid yourself of the suspicion that they also contain a hidden pocket, serving some mysterious purpose. In an airman's kit there are items, which, as the product of endless experience, are quite perfect. Real works of art. Such are our trousers, the owners of which divide into two parties, according to the way their trousers are worn. The first, more inclined to terrestrial vanity, wear the trouser legs under the flying boots because this looks more elegant. The other, more matter-of-fact party, zip the trousers over the boots with the argument that, when *"Aussteigen"* (alighting from the aircraft - simple code for baling out), one can very easily lose one's boots through aerial somersaults, unless they have previously been secured by the all-enveloping trouser-legs. Experience shows that a parachute descent in winter is even more unpleasant when one has to swing down to wintery earth from 6,000 metres - Montblanc is lower! - with temperatures to match, but in socks or bare feet. The upper part of the body is encased in an ingeniously constructed and lined jerkin or fur waistcoat. Only the scarf, in its different material, colour or folds, betrays the effort to achieve a personal touch.'

Clausen sees the funny side of the tough job that has to be done. He writes: 'Now there they all stood. Officers and other ranks. Small and large, fat and thin. Soldiers have a sensitive feeling for the point where pathos becomes bathos. There stood a small *Leutnant* with a mischievous Heinz Rühmann[7]-like face. His effort to land on the

[7] - *Heinz Rühmann - A famous German comedy actor who featured in many films in the thiries and forties including 'Die Drei von der Tankstelle' (The Three from the Petrol Station) and 'Quax der Bruchpilot' (Wrecking Pilot) in which he did much of his own flying. He was a qualified pilot and was on the reserve list. He enjoys good health and at the time of writing he is in his nineties.*

Reichsautobahn with a worn out, (actually shot to pieces) undercarriage and his last drop of petrol, had rewarded him with a foot encased in plaster for four weeks. He enjoyed satirising his own future with the standard stirring sentence: "Tight lipped. Men who will risk their all." No, the night fighters did not look so dramatic. They were no living war memorials, but the decent faces of young men from all the German provinces. Strong and bold, good natured and mischievous, nervous and imperturbable, self controlled, but also boys' faces which unconsciously reflected every excitation. Paradoxically, one might have said: common to all of them was their diversity, that particular and distinctive thing which characteristically we are only accustomed to ascribe to the personality.'

How is such a night fighter crew put together and what sort of understanding is there between the men? The war correspondent explains it thus: 'You repeatedly notice the differences within a crew, which in night fighters consists of several men. Especially when the right mix has been achieved, it seems as if, quite instinctively, they carry out a kind of supplementary by-election between themselves. The nervous one chums up with the intelligent and phlegmatic, the bold one with the sensitive. It is like a kind of human gear box: the strengths of one mesh into the neutral spaces of the other. In this way, a new body with enhanced capabilities is created. With its occupants, the aircraft forms a new organism, in which the functions of tracking and destroying combine sensibly and in concentrated form. It is probably the highest form in which man and machine have combined to destroy the enemy.'

As was mentioned at the beginning of this chapter, the war correspondent also knew the man to whom this book is dedicated. Clausen writes: 'Among the pairs of opposites I have mentioned, I was particularly struck by *Major* Prinz zu Sayn-Wittgenstein, holder of the Iron Cross with Oak Leaves, and his wireless operator. It was in November. The whole *Geschwader* was on parade in front of the hangars, without gloves or greatcoats, on a pretty cold day. We were awaiting an inspection by the *Reichsmarschall* (Göring) whose arrival was delayed. They were all frozen to the marrow, but putting a brave face on it. In the front rank, comprising only pilots, *Major* Prinz zu Sayn-Wittgenstein stood on the flank of the *Gruppe* he led. Slight and slim, and gritting his teeth to avoid betraying the fact that he was frozen, he radiated a strange determined state of concentration. He was a tough fighter whose whole being seemed to concentrate itself, like a beam, on one point, night fighting! Flying, hunting, shooting down!

There is a story that he once jumped out of a car to board his aircraft, ready for take off, when one boot stuck fast. Impatiently, he yanked his foot out of the boot and flew for four hours, in icy conditions, with his foot, only covered by a silk sock, on the rudder bar. He was surely a man obsessed. For this kind of man, there is hardly another way of fulfilling his existence than in a situation where everything is at stake. Man invents machines, but it often seems that the machines challenge those people who are their equals, so that something new and complete emerges, as from horse and rider. At that inspection the then wireless operator of his aircraft stood in the second rank behind the Prinz. Chubby, with a pleasant round face, looking jovial and good natured. One could well have imagined him as the young, friendly and solicitous landlord of a *Weinstube* in the *Palatinate*[8]. But this outer face concealed an intelligence out of the ordinary and great knowledge.' (Clausen is referring to the present Dr Eng Herbert Kümmritz, to whom we are indebted for the section on the technical aspects of night fighting.)

Clausen devotes a whole chapter to the parachute, its advantages and its foibles: 'Military wisdom is simple;

[8] - *Palatinate - Rural Central Germany*

"The fing must sit proper or you're in the shit," warned the *Obergefreiter* at the parachute school, as he fitted my parachute harness. Pearl of wisdom! After you have baled out and your groping hand has found the release buckle, there is a second of terror "when you think of all your relations". Will it open or not? Until a whiplash jerks the body. The parachute is open. In a sudden silence which seems to lie on the far side of all experienced soundlessness, you hang down, swinging widely and feel blissfully happy: the harness is holding. This dear, good harness, so often regarded as a nuisance and quietly cursed when flying in a narrow aeroplane. What a sense of well-being when you push open the cabin roof after landing, turn the ingenious buckle, which holds all the parts of the harness over your chest, to the left, slap it hard with the flat of your hand and the claustrophobic straps fall off your shoulders and thighs, like the bonds of a liberated slave. Yes, the parachute! It is more than a technical necessity, more than a lifebelt on board ship. You wear it on your chest, on your back or like a cushion, exactly under the seat of your pants. What a dependable friend! How much strength it exudes when you are swinging miles above the earth at night. At such times, you think in dumb admiration of the first flyers of the last World War, who still flew without a parachute and who were beyond hope of rescue if the aircraft began to wallow under the heavy weight of sudden icing and then went into a vertical spin; if an engine burst into flames, or if the machine was shot up in an air battle. In those many adventurous and often gruesome situations, in which a thoroughbred instrument like an aircraft, still responding smoothly to every pressure on the control column and every pull on a lever, is suddenly turned into a wreck, a parachute nowadays is the only salvation for the crew. Then it is an enormous silk 'chute, ingeniously folded down to the size of a portable typewriter, which stands between life and death. All existence is concentrated on the simple flat buckle on the chest, the flyer's "emergency brake".

Wittgenstein prepares for a night sortie.

There are famous and successful night fighters who have never had to bale out, whereas for others, the parachute has often been the last salvation. Some of our night fighter pilots, incidentally, are so well known among the British that captured British flyers often ask whether they were, at least, shot down by an ace night fighter pilot. That appears honourable to them. This only by the way. So long as it is not yet "criminal" - as a favourite expression for all embarrassing flying situations runs - you do not think of your parachute very much and, rather, find the heavy thing burdensome. But I remember, as if it were today, the very moment when an invisible halo seemed to glow around my parachute. We had taken off on a rainy night, despite the frightful weather, towards the incoming enemy bomber formations. Near Brunswick, my pilot, *Hauptmann* Peters, saw the first four engined bomber. He opened fire and the burning Lancaster disappeared into the clouds. Unfortunately, we were unable to confirm that it hit the ground. So it was only a "probable" which would not be counted as a "kill". Then, in the next half hour, there were two further "kills". All the ammunition had gone since, with the second "kill", there was an air battle lasting almost ten minutes before it blew up.

We set course for our home station. *Hauptmann* Peters suddenly shouted: "Damn, the red lights have come up." The red lights were an optical warning that there was only enough fuel left for a certain flying time. That also meant that, if we had not reached an airfield before time ran out, our only option would be to bale out. On this particular night with a cloud base of 80 metres, there would have been no alternative. We looked at the luminous dials of our watches. "How far to go?" the *Hauptmann* asked the wireless operator. He is still calculating. "We'll just about manage", he opines finally. In such moments it is only a small comfort that similar things often happen. But, involuntarily, everyone checks the fit of his parachute and harness. In night flying how long the minutes drag, until, as now, they start galloping away. Despite that there is plenty of time to think. All the stories occur to you again: where a crew did not succeed in baling out soon enough; where someone was flung, by the high airspeed, into the rudder, or where the parachute tore because the man baling out did not wait until his body, which was vastly accelerated by the headlong speed of the falling aircraft, had reduced its speed to normal terminal velocity. Within grabbing distance there is a small strip of wood. It looks very fragile and harmless. It is edged in red and made visible in the dark by fluorescent paint. "Jettison cabin roof" is printed on it. In such dodgy moments, existence reduces itself to an insignificant point, a small dubious looking lever. Once again you check whether your hand can reach the lever at speed and carefully push the machine gun belt aside. When the order to bale out comes, everything must happen fast; and the pilot jumps last - the ancient prerogative of captains.

Well we landed with those last drops of fuel which have become legendary from countless similar situations. Our tall *Hauptmann* was wringing with sweat. The last twenty minutes had tugged vastly harder at his nerves than shooting down three four-engined bombers and the long air battle. He alone bore responsibility for the valuable aircraft and the crew entrusted to him. Three weeks before - and the memory still scared him - he had shot down two Lancasters at night, but in the process took shots in his fuel tank. Both engines suddenly stopped so he had to order the crew to bale out immediately. Only when his two crewmen had got out, could he think of saving himself.

In between times the machine had stood on its head, and fell at a speed increasing by the second into the pitch black depths. Jettisoning the cabin roof, he could not get out. When he tried to stand up, the phenomenal pressure of the slipstream pushed the upper part of his body and his raised arms backwards, like someone who had been crucified. With a last despairing effort of which, he said, he had never before been capable nor ever would be again, he pushed his arms downwards, inch by inch, against the frightful stream of air until his hands came to rest on the left and right cabin side walls. Then he pushed himself up while, as if in a frightful dream, he could read off from the altimeter how soon the machine would hit the ground. And suddenly the slipstream sucked him out of the aircraft. As he was hurled in huge somersaults through the air, he could not wait until his body slowed down to normal velocity but had to pull the rip cord at once and survive for a second, which seemed like an eternity, until the parachute opened and he experienced the indescribable bliss of feeling safe: the body and the parachute had stood up to the tremendous pressure.'

Now becoming a bit emotional, war correspondent Clausen closes this chapter on night fighting with the two following paragraphs, in which he draws together the feelings about survival experienced by the night fighters, just as, right inside, Prinz Wittgenstein might have felt from time to time, even if he did not talk about it.

'In seconds like that the life thus regained roars back into us with heart stretching fullness, like a waterfall. The scent and sweetness of simple existence - do we know before such an experience what life, what the simple wave-breaking experience of breathing in and out means? - fill the inner life like an intoxicating tank. One is truly full of life. Often after such experiences when life was gifted anew we observe, both in ourselves and in our comrades, an unusually euphoric loquaciousness. One laughs for no reason and shows in gesticulation, expression and speech all the symptoms of slight drunkenness.

Drunk simply on life! Ah, and that is when you first properly understand the lines: "If you do not put your life on the line, your life will never be won." Didn't we sing that in chorus as boys, and as recruits, filled with a strange elation, only sensing but far removed from that ethereal realisation which is only born on that invisible borderline where life and death flow into each other.'

'The Deadly Elements' is Clausen's heading for his next chapter, which describes in journalistic form circumstances related to night fighting, about which Dr Eng Kümmritz has written from a purely technical point of view.

Clausen's piece begins: 'Nights of destruction? We experienced them on leave from the front when bombs and fire, like the end of the world, tore the stone fabric of our home towns to shreds. Never shall we forget the wide, frightened eyes, their courage wrung from fear, their despair and their bravery.'

Clausen then describes the weather conditions in which the battle had to be fought and in this respect supplements Kümmmritz's accounts: Nights of destruction - how differently we experienced them from the air. 'Compelled by grim losses, the enemy has long since switched to continue attacking only when the weather has closed down over Germany. For the most part it is made more difficult for the attacking bombers to achieve effective destruction, but this kind of weather also demands the ultimate effort from our defence. When the Met briefing takes place in the evening, the so arid sounding data comes out, cloud ceiling 50 - 80 metres, icing at all levels up to a ceiling of 5,000 metres, only a few diversion airfields, there and there - then the crews look at one another dumbly. This look says it will be "criminal".

If the engine or wireless equipment fails in daylight 200 metres after take off, you have a quick look round and make a wheels-up landing in the nearest field. At night, from autumn till spring, a technical failure can mean death. Not to mention icing up! It is very significant when a night fighter pilot, who has already gone through many an air battle, countless difficult take-offs, and even more dangerous landings at night, admits that there is nothing he fears as much as icing. The battle with icing is always a bitter game with death.

This is what happens. Up top, high above the layers of dangerous icing, come the enemy bombers from their home bases which are clear today. The night fighter has taken off. For a few seconds he could still see the red marker lights on the perimeter of the airfield; these have already paled in the mist and disappeared. The machine climbs through the grey, dark swirl of cloud. The wing tips are hardly visible any more. What did the meteorologist say: upper limit of cloud at 5,000 metres! But at a 1,000 metres icing has already begun. This time quite gradually. The machine's rate of climb drops off. Higher and higher, the pilot's body is already damp with sweat.

Aren't we banking to the right? he thinks with sudden fright. Instinctively he leans to the left as if this would correct the tilt. But his reason forbids the hands on the control column to correct the imagined tilt. He takes another look at the instruments. According to these, the machine is flying absolutely horizontal. But his instinct whispers: Perhaps the instruments are no longer accurate. This is the start of a nerve-racking inner struggle which nearly always occurs when flying blind: the conflict between the personal sense of balance, which blind flying experience shows to be deceptive, and the instruments. Feeling demands: Believe me, not your instruments. He swears it to himself, calls all tried and tested experience in aid, forces himself only to believe the instruments and not to look to left or right. And yet it remains a hard fight.

At 5,000 metres, the icing has become so heavy that he considers going down again into layers of warmer air. He is already far out to sea. It's clear, ahead there's a new bad weather front approaching! Better go back, but he cannot risk turning on to a reciprocal course because the heavily iced machine, with its severely impaired handling characteristics, could crash in the process.

He knows his wireless operator and air gunner are behind him. They have a sense of foreboding but do not know what the pilot knows. So, go on climbing. There! Isn't that the first stars shining through the thinning cloud? Another 1,000 metres and he should be out of it. Then they will have made it. If the icing gets any thicker in the last 1,000 metres, then they will have had it. A parachute will be no use. The sea is cold; nobody can survive in it for longer than an hour. A thousand thoughts crowd in on him. Quietly he curses to himself. "What's up?" asks the wireless operator on the intercom. "Oh, nothing, we'll soon be through," the pilot answers and tries very hard to sound relaxed. But the operator knows him, they have been flying together for a long time. He keeps looking anxiously at the increasing layer of ice on the wing sections. Nor can he fail to hear when pieces of ice, which have broken away from the propeller, rattle against the cabin windows.

But at long last they are through. In open sky at last. Everything to come seems easy to them. Who cares about enemy bombers and night fighters, or the most dangerous anti-aircraft free-fire zones, or the air battle, after the heavenly elements have freed them from their icy embrace.

They are not yet thinking about the landing and its perils. One unlucky shot in the wireless set, the only means of navigating on nights when you cannot see the ground, and all is lost. How often the night fighters have that experience! Then comes the difficult decision: shall we bale out, or try to land all the same? You no longer know exactly where you are. Still over the plain or already over the mountains? Try to push on down below the mist. The cloud base is just 50 metres above ground level. Perhaps the pilot will be lucky and emerge from the cloud right above the plain! But, even then, the mortal danger would not yet be overcome. Where is there an airfield? If you are flying at some hundreds of kilometres an hour through the darkness, the smallest of hills, a high voltage pylon, or a chimney, would mean sudden destruction.

These are not carefully chosen, rare, cases but the daily bread of the night fighter. From autumn through till spring, he has to take off in storm conditions which are a source of mortal danger from take-off to landing. If we have good flying weather the enemy, who has become more cautious, does not fly in. As a result practically every night operation is a bad weather operation. There are silent tests of courage which stretch people to the uttermost limit but bring no decorations. No outsider has the faintest idea what nervous tension and how many battles are hiding behind the simple formulation of the weather forecast: "In spite of bad weather conditions..." If one wants to explain this clearly to the layman, one easily runs into the danger of becoming emotional, because genuine emotion lurks behind these nightly operations. Since real servicemen are very sensitive in this area, they have developed a particular technique in their colloquial speech, often to conceal everything dramatic in brutal language, or to dismiss it with irony or sarcasm.'

One of the most gripping accounts ever written about night fighting was again produced by Clausen, the war correspondent. Under the heading, 'Now for the next one!' he describes the detail of operations, such as were experienced almost nightly between 1942 and 1944 by Prinz Wittgenstein. 'The next one,' in this case, is the next enemy to be shot at. Clausen, who, even as a war correspondent, flew regularly on operations, first describes preparations for take-off.

'Order to take-off. Two minutes later we are standing in the hanger. Lights flare up and the big doors are pushed open. We get ready. Faint excitement runs through the nerves like a weak electric current. So now on with the life jacket. Collar up, parachute harness over the shoulders, collar down again, harness secured in lock on chest. Is everything fitting properly? Yes, we climb into the aircraft. Our low pitched cabin is tight at the elbows. I sit back-to-back with the wireless operator, and we have to sit at a slight angle in order to mesh in. While he checks his instruments, he makes one or two unfitting observations in his softly drawn out Rhineland intonation. He has a granite sense of humour.

Right, now put the breathing mask on, just to test it and draw a deep breath. The oxygen line is in order. It is true that dying at high altitude from a shortage of oxygen is a gentle death, but inglorious. The two machine guns protecting our back are cocked, with safety catch on. Now put on the helmet with the headphones sewn in over the ears. The two ivory smooth throat microphones are fixed over the larynx with press studs. We taxi towards take-off. Press on the small button to the left and a new audio world opens up: it squeaks, bleeps, resounds and speaks gobbledegook until the wireless operator has tamed this confused world of sound and made it serviceable.'

Clausen goes on to describe how his first night operation went: 'All the manual aspects of the job are clear to the point of photographic accuracy. Everything else remained in the memory like an impressionist painting. Looked at from close to, it glows in a confusion of paint blobs; it is only when seen from a distance that the picture sorts itself out and shows its meaning. It is always exciting when one knows: We're just off. As if the oscillatory system of nerves was switching to another wavelength. You receive (oscillations) more quickly, more intensively and more sensitively. And the frequency changes for a second time immediately after take-off. The breathing becomes more shallow and the irrevocable takes us into its peaceful landscape, into the peace of a great spatial order. A new focus forms.

Take-off! We fly into the mist. Climb. Climb. Higher and higher. At 2,500 metres *Hauptmann* Peters shouts:

"Breathing masks on!" On the intercom, a nice kind of permanent telephone connection between us three occupants, the voices sound deeper and more guttural than in reality. On my first flights I hardly understood a word. It takes time for the ear to accustom itself. Now we are above the clouds. The night is moonless and dark. Over the grey cloud banks which we have left far below, the star studded dome of the endlessly distant heavens curves upward. We are 6,000 metres up, beneath us only velvet grey, but against the lighter sky you can at least see something. Through the headset I can hear the directions of the ground station controlling us. They inform us continually where the leading enemy aircraft are and where they are heading. Which town will he attack today? There's no clue at the moment. The only certainty is that they will not stick to their present course but will attack at some other point.

Suddenly, the sky springs to life. In the distance the deep cloud landscape lights up. Searchlights are probing the underside of the cloud. Small pin point stars flare up and die at once: The Flak is firing in that direction.

Hauptmann Peters changes course. Something must be happening over there. We have reached the point in the flight where everything hangs on the pilot's instinct. This instinct has honed itself in the course of many operations and has become like that of a hunter. With many of our famous night fighter pilots, this trait is so marked that they nearly always find enemy aircraft, almost with the assurance of a sleepwalker. You must not imagine that the often quoted bomber stream is also dense. In such a stream the distance between individual four engined bombers, in terms of height and depth, is still several kilometres. If you are unlucky, you can fly in the "stream" and yet not get a single enemy in front of your cannons. What is that on the horizon to the right? Like a rising full moon, a red ball glows. "Let's have a look", growls *Hauptmann* Peters and changes course towards the, as yet inexplicable, light signal. While he is scanning the airspace in front of our aircraft, I look towards the rear. The wireless operator is quietly tinkering with mysterious instruments. It has turned cold. Outside it is minus 53 degrees Celsius. If somebody could observe me from outside, he would be obliged to think I was dotty. My head is continually making a wave-shaped circular motion, rather like those exercises the neck. Look down to the right, sideways, forwards, upwards, and then the same to the left. Constantly. From a long way off a shimmering green dot approaches, nearer and nearer. "Down!", I shout, because it could be an enemy night fighter. We put our nose down and continue on our course 200 metres lower. The green dot has disappeared.

But we are on the right track. In front of us, the usual firework display of a night attack is developing. It is still something like 100 kilometres ahead. We know the signs. Suddenly our machine shudders upwards, as if under an unrolling wave. That must be the slipstream of another aircraft flying in front of us. Is it an enemy or a hunting chum? The slipstream was only just noticeable, so the distance must still be quite considerable. Hello, I catch sight of it with a jump, the enormous silhouette of a four engined bomber passes by, slowly intersecting our course, about 200 metres below. A wonderfully exciting feeling. That's him, the enemy, the one we have been looking for, found at last. It floats in dignified silence below. We hang above him, like a bird of prey over its unsuspecting victim. Down there, in the aircraft, enemies sit, tons of parachute mines, high explosive bombs and incendiaries hang in the bomb bays.

I have to control myself, not to shout too loud in the excitement: "*Herr Hauptmann*, one coming from the right, below us". I have not finished speaking before we sideslip down to the right. Naturally, my attention was distracted, so I was lifted out of my seat by the steep dive and taught painfully thereby that the cabin roof was harder than my skull. This is forgotten in the ferocity of the next minute. "There he is, great!" the *Hauptmann* shouts happily. It sounds like the primeval triumphant shout of the hunter, at the first sight of the game at bay. There is a hard thud against the trembling fuselage of our machine. A single burst, but from all our cannon and machine guns. "He's burning, he's burning!" We bank steeply away and now I can see him again. It looks unreal, almost theatrical, as bright flames blaze up from the enormous fuselage of the enemy bomber. The pilot below has already stood his four engined bird on its head, trying to dive out of danger. But we are still breathing down his neck. The cannon thud again and you can smell the cordite through your breathing mask. It was the *coup de grâce*. Down there the wing surfaces and engines are now alight. Out of control, the Lancaster dives vertically and disappears into the cloud, which seconds later flushes purple: impact and detonation of the bomb load. He will not bring any more sorrow over the homeland.

"Get moving, the next one," *Hauptmann* Peters hurries himself along. For our tall *Hauptmann* Peters, who can sometimes look like a scholar, this is not a murderous job. He wants to shoot the enemy down before he can drop his bombs. He does not derive so much pleasure from shooting them down on their way home. So he whips up his machine higher and further. I can tell from his short exclamations how much the hunt is exciting him.

A human being can show so many sides to his character! This morning I found him in his room, very unmilitary with a towel round his neck while the station barber gave him a trim. He had a much read book on his knee. God, it's Zarathustra. He can quote an astonishing amount from this book. But not the sort of thing commonplace readers would sideline in Zarathustra. But, for the moment, old Nietzsche has long since been stashed away in his spiritual luggage, because I suddenly hear him shout: "There's another one!" Our engines have to give their all. I strain to look to the rear. But now we are at it. Only this time it takes seven attacks until the enemy, diving to escape, is torn to bits by a powerful explosion just above the cloud. A single parachute, showing white in the light of the explosion, swings downwards.

The ammunition is exhausted. The time from the first encounter to the last "kill" seems endlessly long but, in fact, it was only 23 minutes. We are flying home. Hundreds of searchlights illuminate the cloud beneath us like a gigantic shroud. The attack on the brave town nears its end. A few blood red cascades of fireworks trickle down. Large white flares form mysterious roads in the heavenly landscape which, strangely frozen, only gives an inkling of the flying forces of destruction. An hour later we have landed. An endless feeling of wellbeing: kind, dear earth under your feet. Silently night's curtains glide together in front of the blazing drama. What a silence! Have all our chums landed? Yes, all safely down. That is a good feeling.'

Clausen closed this chapter of his report with the following observations: 'Back in the huts. Slowly, all becomes quiet. The last lights go out. After an operation you think of so many things while waiting for fugitive sleep. Perhaps we shall not realise the significance of many events in our war until many years later, when they are stripped of their almost frightful horror. How much, which is superficially contradictory, can the great life keep in balance, with weights of which we are ignorant. We have hunted enemy bombers over our towns on dark nights; over our towns, in which people dear to us live, and whose buildings in the shape of a thousand treasures of the past are dear to us, and which reflect the being and longing of our forefathers. Yet despite this there was hardly one of us whom the diabolical magnificence, with which the monstrous spectacle of a night attack develops, did not at times shake with sheer horror. The destruction does not sicken our souls because we have learned to renounce everything for the sake of a goal. Nor do we need any theological confirmation to know that the work of man is all transitory. Only the spirit and that mysterious, loving, life force, which destroys the flowers in the autumn only to give birth to thousands of new ones in the spring, are eternal. It is not only in the words of the classics that nature causes new life to bloom in the ruins. So one day new urban landscapes will rise up which will be able to reflect our new German existence. It is also not a cheap attempt to make a virtue of necessity if we perceive that out of this great trial the most marvellous artistic forces can be liberated, if we have a positive attitude to our life and our fate.'

So much for Clausen, generous, ranging far and readily remembered. Now what he says here is surely quite the mildest form of rallying slogan, usual in those days. Between the lines you can already read a healthy measure of scepticism, and Clausen concentrates completely on his mission, night fighting. At all events, the "final" victory does not figure in his reports.

However, in another chapter, this war correspondent once more took a close look at Prinz Wittgenstein and his objectives. It is the comparison between Wittgenstein and *Major* Lent. Under the title 'Hunt the Laurel,' Clausen wrote:

The tally of 'Kills' are recorded on the tail of the Ju.88.

'This is what the wonders of war look like. But we need to look for them not only there where, once again, fate mercifully closes doors which were already open. Sometimes this fate chooses death as the last allegory for the significance of a life.

In the Middle Ages when a young warrior went into the field, he prayed for fame and honour. In beautiful naïvety. The Schliefen saying, *"Mehr sein als scheinen"* (Be more than you appear to be), would at that time, have appeared differently to a young warrior than it does to us. His thirst for fame was, for him, something obviously positive. Not so in the people's armies of the world wars of our time. How our military style has changed! Be the ambition, the thirsting after fame and distinction, ever so strong in a soldier - it conforms with his style to let nothing of these leak to the outside.

With the night fighters it is the same as with the day fighters. The sum of success is clear from the number of enemy aircraft shot down. So from time to time there is a silent competition running between a fair number of great "shooters" among the night fighters. For months *Major* Prince zu Sayn-Wittgenstein trailed close behind *Major* Lent who led the field with the highest number of night "kills". That is no false ambition. Against whom should one measure oneself, if not the best?

Since the previous summer the number of "kills" achieved by both pilots has been increasing with every sortie. A silent drama. Many times they shot not just one but two, three, four and even five, four-engined bombers out of the sky in one night. If it sometimes looked as if the Prinz zu Sayn-Wittgenstein was close to catching up with his comrade, Lent, in the very next night operation, Lent would again surge ahead. Then, at the end of January 1944, came Wittgenstein's last battle. In barely an hour, he shot down five Lancasters. For the first time, he had succeeded in topping the table of aircraft shot down. Eighty-three "kills". He could not know this for certain, since Lent too was on operations that night. But perhaps he suspected it with great pride before he died the flyer's death. His crew were able to bale out. Thus Wittgenstein did not live to be invested with the Swords to the Oak Leaves of the Knight's Cross. Clausen ends this part of his war report with the following reflections: 'Since the mortal part of us is unimportant but the substance is, and because a secret but inexorable law prescribes to every one of us how we can fulfil our life's work in the purest way, the significance of such a death, which at a superficial glance appears quite senseless, shines out clearly from the dark fates of this war.'

So much for the descriptions by a man who, as a journalist during the war, wrote in masterly fashion about the war and, in the process, lost his life.

Wittgenstein at a comrade's grave.

CHAPTER SIX

AIR BATTLES

At the beginning of his service as a fighter pilot Wittgenstein was also in action on the Eastern Front. Even at that time Herbert Kümmritz, as wireless operator, was a member of the crew. Kümmritz has written a story about this period which shows that he was not only a technician. The story is dedicated to Prinz Wittgenstein and entitled 'Die kleine Nachtmusik' (the little night music).

'We three men of the Wittgenstein crew obeyed the order to take off in an unusual way, which was not altogether without danger. Instead of hurrying to the machine by a direct route at the double, we ran and jumped from trench to trench and dugout to dug out, at pains to keep out of the way of falling bombs. The bombs fell sporadically and were widely distributed, but all the same, they fell. "The daft buggers," cursed the flight engineer. A nearby impact made him jump and silenced him.

Naturally, fear also played a part, a fear different from the one which used to disappear as the aircraft taxied just before take-off. The idea that if you going to die would mean being killed in an air battle, or somehow perishing with the aircraft, made thoughts of being killed by a bomb seem almost crazy. While we two, the wireless operator and the flight engineer, were intensively occupied with ourselves and thinking of our own lives, the pilot seemed above all to be motivated by concern for the aircraft standing ready for take-off, "I hope it hasn't copped any splinters," he growled shortly.

As we got close to the aircraft, the No 1 of the ground crew, a typical Berliner, popped up. He had been sheltering from the bombs in a hollow patch of ground, but not without keeping the aircraft under constant observation. "All OK, *Herr Hauptmann*, the machine hasn't copped it, you can take off. If a bomb had gone off, I wouldn't be alive." In his words was a tinge of the arrogance of *Luftwaffe* people who rarely thought of the Russian enemy as being their equal, quite unjustifiably as they were to find out very soon. Anyhow, half reassured, we climbed into our Ju 88 and prepared for take-off with the accustomed speed. Before we had finished all the necessary chores the two engines roared into life and, to the astonishment of those remaining on the ground, the *Hauptmann* tore straight across the airfield, ignoring take off and landing regulations and falling bombs, to the beginning of the runway. As his crew were to some extent used to this, their terror was held in check. Both the relative paucity of falling bombs and the feeling of being safer in the air eased the tension.

Only just airborne the flight mechanic's voice was already warning, "Flak below right." And indeed, flak shells were exploding under the aircraft, partly with a flash, partly leaving black cloudlets, almost a peaceful firework display and yet full of murderous energy. "Those are our 88's firing blind," murmured the pilot, more angry than anxious, and added superfluously, by way of a reference to the drama on the ground, "We must be near the front." And, in reality, that is the front line or, put more accurately, the line of the front, a giant fire-spitting lindworm which spreads itself over the whole breadth of the visible terrain from north to south. To call this a "drama" would be pure blasphemy; there is nothing here essentially worthy of praise or contemplation; there's nothing here which would correspond to anything in normal civilian life; there is something murderous, something frightful beyond measure unfolding here. Armies face each other, struggling like Titans, swallowing up divisions, tanks and guns. The lindworm, whose body comprises thousands of oscillating flashes of fire - exploding shells, bullets and bombs - devours everything.

He is called "*Zitadelle*"[1] - codename for the last great German offensive on the Eastern Front, a grandiose but vain attempt to change the fortune of war in the far flung Russian Empire.

As if to spare the eye from seeing the worst, clouds suddenly interpose themselves, like a curtain, between the aircraft and the turbulent terrain. And it is the clouds which help the enemy go on flying and living. They surround the man who suspects nothing of the mortal threat and, without any defensive movements, hurries away to the East. These facts are registered almost angrily in the fighter. A "certain kill" is escaping. And the Control Station can do nothing else than note painfully: "*Kurier* has overflown the front, break off engagement and return to "*kleine Laterne*" ('small lantern' - code for designated radio beacon).'

"That would have been No 35," said the pilot briefly, with an undertone which betrayed more disappointment than anger. "Have a new *Kurier* for you," said the Fighter Control Officer triumphantly. "Vector..."

And while the hunt gets under way again, demanding of the crew every possible variation of feelings, something strange, something wonderful happens: music, cheerful music emanating, so to speak, from another world mixed itself in, albeit quietly and unobtrusively, with the articulation of war. The aircraft's radio receiver was switched to "Radio Telephony", used as a rule for transmitting brief military reports became, as it were, the conveyor of a message from another world: it sounded contrapuntal to the war torn world, harmonious and graceful, *DIE KLEINE NACHTMUSIK*, evening serenade in G major, magic Mozart music. To judge by the theme - the introductory theme had just ended - the receiver had only missed the first bars of the Allegro. Clear and pure, drowned out only by brief ground control orders which were, however, increasing in intensity, "*Zweimal Lisa, Ente*

[1] - 'Zitadelle' - Citadel - The battle for Kursk salient.

800, machen Sie Pauke-Pauke,"[2] the melodies from a nearby forces station inundate the consciousness of the crew directed at the battle. Irritated by the almost painful contrast between the harmonious and ethereal and the brutal and earthly, the pilot asks: "Can't you switch the music off?" To which I, obviously more deeply influenced by the music reply almost joyfully: "No, *Herr Hauptmann*, the forces station is sitting on top of our R/T frequency." However, I could not avoid adding, after looking at the screen: "*Kurier* 300 metres ahead, slightly higher." And so it happened that scattered amongst the uninhibited joy of making music which concludes the first movement of the Serenade, machine guns rattle, the smell of powder permeates the cabin, and an aircraft, the enemy bomber, dissolves itself into flaming torches. The death in the flaming inferno and the celestial music just did not fit together, and yet this was reality, an all too clearly experienced reality; a reality corresponding to the contradictions of a world which had come apart at the seams.

And while the wireless operator noted down the time and place of the "kill" - 2132 hours, 25 kilometres east of Orel - at the same time considering the possibility of a frequency change, the languages of art and war join forces again in the articulation of extreme opposites. In the variety of melodies in the second movement, Andante and Romance, the strings cause the melodies to blossom, driving the introductory theme right to its climax - directions from the Control Station break in, now concentrated but no longer excited. The unknown voice who, in the preliminary stages of the air battle, fatefully shared the decision over life and death, points out, downright euphorically, two *Kuriers* who, about to bomb the German sector of the front, are on the point of crossing

----

[2] - Coded message: *"Zweimal* (turn 20°) *Lisa (Links* - left), *Ente* (Duck - target) *800* (metres range), *machen Sie Pauke-Pauke* (attack - fire)."

our path. The guns were already reloaded, so it required only brief course corrections from the wireless operator to bring the fighter into its firing position. And again the scene concentrated itself into an ominous complexity: searchlight beams seeking the aircraft, anti-aircraft shells exploding, hunters and prey equally threatening; below, the front bubbled and boiled, tracer trails are born, develop in the air to become pearls of death, clinging tightly to the enemy and blowing him up. And all this lifted out of reality by Mozart. Oh God, how much understanding You demand of us.

By the beginning of the third movement - Allegretto, Minuet and Trio - this phase of the battle was over; both Russian bombers were smouldering on the ground, providing their crews with a funeral pyre of unusual dimensions if they were unable to bale out. Even more than habit and the sense of duty which turn life, being dashed to the ground, into an abstraction of the necessity to shoot down an enemy, it was the seduction of the music which made one forget all this, fire, crash and death. Minuet - don't the couples dance in wigs, parading the princely court and gallantry, made magic by candlelight and nobility? Were these not sounds, which much, much later bewitched audiences in the concert halls of the world, and in the palaces and residencies of Europe? Memories were stirred but overtaken, all too quickly, by the reality of war. The scenery refused to change. And as the fourth movement, the Rondo, resounded, sparkling and witty, piquant and boisterous, the death dealing routine, which roused the crew to excitement, repeated itself: approach, attack, shoot down! This time it was an enemy aircraft which gave me problems in locating it on radar, and which was almost rammed by our heavy fighter. "That nearly went wrong," said the pilot with relief as he pointed out the parachute which offered the enemy a way back to life. He was swinging towards the witches' cauldron of the 'Zitadelle', but he was alive.

The Rondo came to an end after letting the

cheerfulness of the main theme swell up again - the serenade faded away. The strings ceded sole mastery to the language of war. We, the crew of the fighter, torn hither and thither between the extremities of life like wanderers between two worlds, were downright relieved. Henceforth, we could pursue our death dealing trade unchallenged, without losing ourselves in the magic of the music. The hunt continues!'

From the *Wehrmacht communiqué* of 25 July 1943: 'Last night Prinz zu Sayn-Wittgenstein and his crew successfully shot down 7 Russian aircraft. This is, hitherto, the highest number shot down in a single night.' There was no mention of Mozart. The serenade was reduced to our cannon and machine guns.

******

Alexander Brosch, an officer in the *Bundeswehr*, has recorded the life of Prinz Wittgenstein and its highlights. Let us follow his account again, as at the beginning of this book: In January 1942 Prinz Wittgenstein transferred to night fighters as a pilot. His mother explained the reason for the transfer: 'He realised that bombing was going to bring too many casualties to the civilian population.' He himself had said - as quoted earlier - that night fighting was the most difficult, but also the highest level of flying. On the night of 6/7 May 1942 he shot down his first enemy aircraft. Until August 1942, Wittgenstein fought as a *Kapitän* in 9. *Staffel* of *Geschwader 2* in the Netherlands, then in Germany. In October 1942, after shooting down 22 he was decorated by *Generalleutnant* Kammhuber, *Chef der Nachtjäger,* with the *Ritterkreuz[3].*

After this Wittgenstein became *Kommandeur* of *IV. Gruppe / Nachtjagdgeschwader 5*, later *I. Gruppe / Nachtjagdgeschwader 100*. Wittgenstein's delicate state of health crops up repeatedly in these difficult days of the

[3] - *Ritterkreuz - Knight's Cross of the Iron Cross.*

In October 1942 Prinz Wittgenstein was invested with the Knight's Cross. He later dedicated the picture to one of his former superiors, Oberst Weiss.

war. In February/March 1943, for example, he had to go into hospital with a stomach problem, but soon recovered. In April/May he was based at Insterburg in East Prussia, operating against incoming Russian aircraft. He was then, between times, in Döberitz and Rennes (France) where he was defending the U-boat pens. Then he was transferred to the Netherlands, and, ultimately, to Russia. On 25 July 1943 he achieved his best success in a day with 7 'kills'. From August until November 1943 he led *II. Gruppe / Nachtjagdgeschwader 3* in Schleswig. In September 1943, after 59 'kills', he was invested with the *Eichenlaub* (Oak Leaves) to the *Ritterkreuz* at Hitler's headquarters.

Crash landing at Doeberitz, April 1943.

In December 1943 he became *Geschwaderkommodore* at Deelen (Netherlands). He found 'a good shoot' there, as he wrote in his last letter to his mother on 15 January 1944. From 1 to 21 January 1944 he shot down a further 15 aircraft and, with a total of 83 aircraft shot down, reached the night fighters' top score. On 21 January 1944 Prinz Wittgenstein was killed. Brosch writes: 'This is why

I try, wherever I can, to ensure that this airman, who stood out both in achievement and bearing, is never forgotten.' A separate chapter will later give an account of his death; this is based mainly on the statements of his wireless operator, Ostheimer, who survived being shot down.

CHAPTER SEVEN

GESCHWADERKOMMODORE

Let us insert an assessment, by the author, of the last post occupied by Wittgenstein. As a young *Major*, he became a *Geschwaderkommodore*, an appointment usually held by an *Oberst* (full Colonel). The more senior air force commander operates from his Headquarters, but not so the *Geschwaderkommodore*. He himself leads in the air, piloting his own aircraft. That is valid for operating as a group flying in formation, however, the night fighters are individualists. The night fighters are familiar with cooperation via radio over large distances, but are dependent on the performance of the individual and the attacking spirit of everyone in a lonely position. Bravery is not negotiable. The brave man overcomes his instinct for self-preservation and fights to the point where his life is on the line. The *Geschwaderkommodore* is a model, he is looked up to.

Wittgenstein, despite his frail constitution, demanded dangerous top performances from himself. He was an exciting individual fighter whose men were inspired by his performance. In the course of this he invented, skilfully and hunter-like, his own methods of attack and could, by virtue of his successes and courage, speak frankly to his superiors. He was everything other than a compliant subordinate.

To call him the father of his men, or a theoretician would be to idealise him. Anyone like him who lived feverishly from one operation to the next in high nervous tension has little time for training, duty rosters, supply and disciplinary questions. Understandably, since he had no more than the knowledge of humankind and experience of a 27 year old.

Wittgenstein the leader.

Wittgenstein led by his example and was a pioneer, a pathfinder, a Leonidas at Thermopolae. To a Hotspur like him the higher command gave an older, experienced staff officer who took over the management of the *Geschwader* on the ground. There are ample historical examples of such a combination. To mention one, in 1773 Friedrich Wilhelm I placed the experienced *Oberstleutnant* von Bredau alongside his son with the task of keeping an eye on order and 'to instil in the Crown Prince good judgement, by reasoned presentation and a good example.'

If one wishes to project soldierly virtues into the future, one should regard the bravery demonstrated in the case of Wittgenstein as a timeless virtue. It is in no way inferior to civil courage. Wittgenstein was the born fighter pilot, a sensitive hand-to-hand battler, an autodidact, a lone wolf. Signs of anxiety from his body - and even he was not spared these - were overcome by his strength of will.

When on the attack he was seized by a *coup de foudre[1]*. Determined to perform at his best he touched neither alcohol nor nicotine and took carefully concentrated food, carotene for sharp vision, oxygen supplement while still on the ground and fluid at high altitudes to balance out the loss caused by psychological and physical exertion.

His withdrawnness indicated unconscious relaxation through self-hypnosis, control and relaxation of the nerves with the purpose of 'recharging the batteries'. His fund of steadfast inner composure was, in his case, to be found in the cohesion of the family. Self discipline came from the same source. And yet he went too far. In the long run his health could not keep pace with the demands which he placed on himself. Stress, strain, pressure to do well, hectic rush, haste, noise, confinement and worry took their toll.

But the aristocratic Wittgenstein, belonging to the elite by virtue of his ability and character, achieved an astonishing performance as a flyer, which made him capable and justified him in pointing the way towards new tactical methods in night fighting, based on his personal example. Through this he became the centre point of a group of kindred spirits and belonged, in the sense meant by Wilhelm Röpke, to the 'self evident nobility'.

Military discipline was subjected to a particular interpretation by him, the non-conformist star achiever. Instead of an uncompromising order, which demands a quite definite reaction without any if's or but's, there was an expectation of success. People let him have his own way. The order was to be carried out in spirit. In carrying out the order, he was given the room to manoeuvre he claimed for himself. The Hitler Youth certified him as being a loyal comrade, an honourable character and a 'born leader', with similar talents in military sports and

[1] - *coup de foudre - French - Thunderbolt.*

*A face changes: the 27 year old Major at
the beginning of 1944. Opposite - the 22
year old Leutnant.*

faultless organisation of expeditions and camps. Years
later, war correspondent Clausen, who has already been
mentioned numerous times, saw him on that November day
when the troops were waiting for *Reichsmarschall* Göring,
and Wittgenstein did not want to show that he was
freezing. Clausen wrote: 'Wittgenstein appears slim,
almost gaunt, overbred and as thin skinned as a
thoroughbred horse.' He seldom laughs, rather gives an
ironic smile. As we have already seen his health repeatedly
caused him difficulties. 'You must not take so much out of
yourself, otherwise one fine day you will fold up
completely!' the *Kommandeur* of *4. Jagddivision* warned
him in 1943.

Let us quote another passage from Alexander Brosch's

biographical note: 'In his company you are struck by his nervous restlessness which only leaves him in his aircraft. Although Wittgenstein is reserved and rather tight-lipped, he can also relax and has good relations with family and friends. If ever he says anything about marriage he speaks of something which is in the future. "In such times," he said, "you wouldn't even tie a dog to you." His still remaining private interests comprise hunting and skiing. He gives himself no rest, glows with passion and obsession, and only eats and sleeps to take off on new night operations.

Undemanding for himself, he gives full support to his subordinates, especially if they have proved themselves in the face of the enemy; he succeeded in getting study leave for his wireless operator, Kümmritz. The Prinz hardly takes any part in the life of the officers' mess. He is self critical, knows when he is in the wrong, shows gratitude and always stresses that, "... others that nobody talks about, who have not once been decorated, who were perhaps destined to perish in some muddy Russian shell hole, were far greater heroes than he was." (As his mother quotes him).

CHAPTER EIGHT

CRITICAL DISTANCE

At some time in the course of the years Prinz Wittgenstein's private attitude must have changed. It is certainly wrong to build him up posthumously as a resistance fighter. But there are a few indications which at least suggest that, towards the end of his life in January 1944, he was more than critical towards the regime. Writing about this period, his mother said: 'He had grown up mainly in Switzerland and while there had loved and idealised the German people from afar. The more Germany was attacked in speech and print the more he loved it. He was a member of the Hitler Youth, and saw in Hitler somebody who believed in Germany. When he recognized from close to what he had honoured and admired from afar, the National Socialist Party, he saw everywhere, with his mature, critical and sober intellect, the human, the all too human side of things: from this time on he devoted his personal good fortune, his carefree youth, his health and his strength to one single goal, the victory of Germany.'

His mother rounds off this part off her observations with the following sentences: 'He was boundlessly disillusioned and boundlessly disappointed. In 1943 he contemplated the thought of shooting Hitler. It was only out of a sense of honour and duty that Heinrich went on fighting, carried along by the ambition to overtake *Major* Lent in his score of enemy aircraft shot down.'

The change in Prinz Wittgenstein was clear from a letter he wrote on 12 September 1943 from Hamburg to his parents in Switzerland. In it he says, 'Many thanks for the latest letters, which arrive more and more slowly and completely irregularly. A letter which arrived yesterday had been two weeks on the way. One, which I got the day

Wreckage of a British bomber shot down by Wittgenstein.

before yesterday, was exactly four weeks old. The letter with good wishes for my birthday and the "kills" has also just arrived and I thank you very much for it. Apart from that the letters are smeared with a filthy sauce.[1] I think the checkpoints are largely to blame. After having been in action at the front for four years and, happily, having the Oak Leaves, I take that as a pretty dirty trick. As far as I and many others are concerned, these checkpoints have made a considerable contribution to the lowering of morale. Otherwise I am well. It has now, it is true, become markedly colder, but instead of swimming and sailing, I can ride round here and shoot rabbits. In the near future I must go to *Führerhauptquartier*[2] to collect my Oak Leaves.'

[1] - *Author's note: Wittgenstein means the blacking out by the censor.*

[2] - *Führerhauptquartier - Hitler's field headquarters.*

*Wittgenstein inspecting parts of a
bomber which was shot down.*

Here is yet another extract from a letter, which Prinz
Wittgenstein wrote to his parents on 6 October 1943 and
which did not reach them, by way of Italy, until 18
January 1944, three days before his death:
'... for this reason, as I have surely already written, I
spent several days at *Führerhauptquartier* and the
Headquarters of the *Reichsmarschall* (Göring) (to receive
the Oak Leaves). It was very interesting, Mussolini had
just left again. I was there with Nowotny and Rall, at the
moment the leading day fighters. Interestingly, the articles
written about me by war correspondents have been
suppressed by a certain censorship office - with the
exception of the official announcement, which you know

about, and which contains considerable mistakes. Hopefully, I will see you soon. With heartiest greetings, I remain Your Heinrich.'

*Wittgenstein receives the Oak Leaves
to the Iron Cross from Hitler.*

Prinz Wittgenstein had naturally not, by any means, told his parents everything about what he thought and felt. He had to exercise restraint because he knew that every letter going abroad, even to Switzerland, had to go through censorship. As mentioned earlier, he did not want 'to tie even a dog to him in these times.' In spite of that he had a tender link to a young noblewoman, to whom he was, at least spiritually, much closer than his relatives or people around him suspected. Only because he knew, suspected or at least had to face the fact that he would not survive the war, did he not further intensify this relationship.

The young lady, the descendant of Russian emigrants, was Marie Princess Wassiltschikow, affectionately known

With other Luftwaffe officers, who were also decorated,
after presentation of the Oak Leaves at Hitler's Headquarters.
From left to right: Hauptmann Novotny, Hauptmann Rall, Hauptmann
Prinz Wittgenstein and Oberstleutnant von Below, Hitler's ADC.

to her friends as 'Missie'. She survived the nights of the
Berlin bombing as an employee of the German Foreign
Office and wrote a book, *'Berlin Diaries'*, from which the
following passage is taken: '25 January 1944... Tonight I
dined with Count Schulenburg (or "the Ambassador", as he
is known, although there are several of them here).
Midway through dinner he announced casually that
Heinrich Wittgenstein had been killed. I froze. He looked
at me with surprise, as he did not know we were such
close friends. Only a few days ago, in Berlin, Heinrich had
rung me up at the office. He had just been to Hitler's H.Q.
to receive from the hands of *"the Almighty"* the Oak
Leaves to his Knight's Cross. He said on the 'phone *"Ich
war bei unserem Liebling"* ["I have been to see our

darling"] and added that, to his surprise, his pistol had not been removed before he entered *"the Presence"* (as is customary nowadays), so that it might have been possible "to bump him off" right then and there. He went on to elaborate on the subject until I remarked that it might be preferable to continue the conversation elsewhere. When we met a little later he started to speculate about the possibility, next time, of blowing himself up with Hitler when they shook hands. Poor boy, little did he suspect that he had only a few more days to live! And yet he seemed so fragile that I always worried about him. He had become Germany's most successful night fighter, was constantly in action and was clearly worn out. He often spoke of the agony he felt about killing people and how, whenever possible, he tried to hit the enemy plane in such a way that the crew could bale out.' So much for the recollections of the Princess.

*On a ski holiday in 1942 at Kitzbühel
with 'Missie' Wassiltschikow.*

*****

Now we have, perhaps, hurried too quickly into the
year of Wittgenstein's death, 1944. In order to round off
the picture of the man, we should flash back just once
more. Ernst Mees, *Leutnant* and pilot in Wittgenstein's
Nachtjagdgeschwader, recalls: 'Between September and
November 1943, as *Kommandeur* of *II. Gruppe* of the
Nachtjagdgeschwader, Wittgenstein was stationed at Jagel
in Schleswig and fought, with almost daily "kills", to close
with Lent, who was then in the lead and whom he was to
overtake in January 1944. At that time I was *Leutnant* and
pilot in *6. Staffel* and saw the *Kommandeur* virtually every
day at the early evening Met briefing, during the nightly
wait in the Command Post, and at meal times in the mess.
It was noticeable that Wittgenstein hardly ever allowed

At the map table prior to a flight. The aerial battlefield over the low countries and northern Germany is visible behind.

himself to be allocated to the areas subject to ground control (*Himmelbett* system). His Ju 88, marbled in grey and white, was always parked near him, either at his hut or the operations room. When the first reports of approaching bombers came in, he at once located himself in front of the large illuminated situation map in the operations room and was the first to roar off to freelance night fighting over the whole of German national territory, while the other pilots took off for their pre-ordained areas.'

Mees also remembers: 'Prinz Wittgenstein was a *Hauptmann* when I first set eyes on him in the autumn of 1942. The night fighter flying personnel were assembled in Holland on one of the well known night fighter airfields. On this occasion *General der Flieger* Christiansen presented the successful crews with a silver goblet engraved with the date, place and type of the enemy aircraft. He referred in soldierly words to the comet-like series of "kills" achieved by Wittgenstein. The tall figure of the young *Hauptmann* impressed itself on the memory of those present. Everybody who met him again on night time stopovers recognized him immediately.

I remember a conversation in the operations room at Jagel. I was Duty Officer in Charge, a function which had to be filled by all aircrew officers on a regular roster. I was sitting with *Major* Dr Otto Schmidt on the Command Rostrum above the Seeburg plotting table in front of the huge illuminated and wall mounted situation map, on which all aircraft movements were indicated by moving lights.

Major Dr Schmidt was a *Pour le Mérite* (Blue Max) fighter pilot in the First World War and came, like me, from the Saarland, so that we always had something to talk about. Suddenly *Hauptmann* Wittgenstein came in and sat down with us, very impatient because nothing was happening. Dr Schmidt steered the conversation on to monarchy as a type of state, as if a development in this direction was possible in the near future. I remember that Prinz Heinrich said little, and still remained in his shell even when the highly educated *Major der Reserve* (trained lawyer, rider and gifted violinist) hinted that hardly anybody but him, Prinz Wittgenstein, could be considered to represent a new monarchy in Germany. Wittgenstein showed embarrassment, almost anger, at what in those times was a daring statement and opined that others could worry about that problem. Wittgenstein believed that it was a time for everyone to do his duty by the Fatherland.

The Kommandeur was no friend of long commentaries. I believe he hated any kind rhetorical self advertisement. He was always polite, never loud or seeking applause. He never wanted to be at the centre of a group but always, incontestably, was because he would listen and, in the subsequent silence, would either indicate agreement and give a summarised judgement, or express brief, well founded disapproval. When I think of the daily encounters, Prinz Wittgenstein is always fresh in my memory and much more clearly drawn than the other participants whose outlines have blurred in the subsequent four and a half decades.

Wittgenstein did not need to invoke any authority, it surrounded him like an invisible aura. I never heard him talk to one of his officers, or reprimand him, other than in a normal tone of voice.

Wittgenstein had to see the *Reichsmarschall* in Berlin. Was his Ju 88 with the *Schräge Musik* unserviceable, or was it having an engine change? He wanted to fly with the Fieseler Storch and ordered me at short notice, after lunch, to be his co-pilot and fly the machine back from Berlin in the afternoon. Wittgenstein flew straight from Schleswig to the *Reichssportfeld*, directly in front of the Olympic Stadium in Berlin. The course followed the pencil line on the map, a real pleasure trip for night fighter pilots because we were flying by eye at about 50 metres, not only because the Storch had no wireless but also because of the danger from enemy fighters. Wittgenstein flew the small aeroplane "along the line" to the south east past Kiel, over the many faceted 'Switzerland' of Holstein, then past the northern boundary of Lübeck, over the foothills of the Mecklenburg lakes to Schwerin and via Putlitz, Pankow and Fehrbellin to the Reich capital.

He was very interested in the landscape, explained to me peculiarities in its formation, asked even more often about our position or the names of places, rivers and lakes which cropped up. The closer he got to Berlin the more taciturn he became. Apparently the meeting he was attending was to deal with important questions relating to night fighting, weaponry, tactics between searchlight clusters and the marker lights of the enemy Pathfinders. These were the questions to be discussed and on which his opinion, his judgement as an experienced pilot and a highly qualified specialist were required. The Prinz landed right next to the Colosseum-like Olympic Stadium and took his leave without ceremony by handing over the Storch for my immediate return to Schleswig. During this flight together in the slow moving kite, he was loquacious and almost relaxed. I realised how young he really was, in spite of his experiences in air battles, a *Kommandeur* at 27 years of age.'

*****

At this point, it may be appropriate for the Author to chime in again: it is not easy to draw a picture of Wittgenstein. Even the Author who, in carefree peacetime *Leutnant* days, was on friendly terms with him, finds it difficult because Heinrich was not particularly inclined to close relationships. Defiant independence was characteristic of him. More dedicated to his cause than to his name, he went all out for it. For all that he was quiet, reserved and a little sardonic. In stature tall, straight, slim, with a clean cut, narrow head, he was always neat and well turned out, a gentleman. Physically rather weak, delicate bones, in sport he displayed unexpected toughness without being aggressive. On skis he left us all standing.

He had no time for *bonhomie*, but did enjoy good conversation. Very self controlled, he avoided quarrels. Boisterous jollity was not him at all, I never heard him roar with laughter.

In 1938, in peacetime, we were still flying together. He sat, burningly interested, behind me as observer in my open, armoured He 45. It was a biplane from the year dot which was pressed into auxiliary service as a battle plane. Impatient at not being able to fly himself he did everything he could to get to Flying Training School. When something out of the ordinary happened he was there, electrified by what was going on. Then he was seized by the Holy Fire. He could not stand our *Staffelkapitän*; he was too loudmouthed, too self important, too egocentric. The Prinz often disagreed with deployment of the *Staffel* in action and had his own ideas on the subject.

When he achieved his most ardent wish to become a pilot we were split up. He began training and I was transferred to a dive-bomber *Geschwader*.

This book is the Song of Songs of a soldier, a son of his times, Heinrich Prinz zu Sayn-Wittgenstein, an expatriate German child, member of the Hitler Youth, a burning patriot, a soldier with extraordinary merits, deeply affected when, towards the end of 1943, he sensed the coming German defeat.

There are not too many, but very impressive, testimonies about Prinz Wittgenstein. There is, for example, his old school in Freiburg. After Heinrich was awarded his Oak Leaves, his old form master sent him a letter which deserves to be quoted here. Professor Alois Wüst wrote on 11 October 1943: 'Dear *Herr Hauptmann!* The whole Erich Ludendorff School is heartily pleased to hear of your high decoration, which is also a testimonial to your outstanding services in defence of our Fatherland against a particularly determined enemy. At the same time the School is proud to be able to count you among its own. The fact that I am only now writing to you is because we have only just got access to your address through Director Grüninger. From the brief letter, which Director Grüninger showed to us, we gather that despite such outstanding success you still think back to your school, albeit, apparently with a somewhat painful impact.

We were all genuinely pleased that you proved to us that, when put to the test, you were a real man and succeeded in doing such an excellent Matura (Leaving Certificate). That your achievement then must have been preceded by a considerable expenditure of energy today seems just useful. You have proved, in fighting for the Fatherland, that where you are needed you are in a position to achieve remarkable things. We congratulate you not only for that, but are thankful from the bottom of our hearts for your success in inflicting so much damage on the greatest enemy of our innermost homeland and will do so in the future. May a kind Fate always watch over you to the well-being of our Fatherland.'

CHAPTER NINE

WITTGENSTEIN'S DEATH

A man who was probably closest to Prinz Wittgenstein was Friedrich Ostheimer. He was a *Feldwebel* during the war, flew in Wittgenstein's crew and was Kümmritz's successor. Ostheimer survived 16 'kills' with Wittgenstein and the death of his *Kommodore*. After the war he became a dental surgeon.

Ostheimer recalls the time with Prinz Wittgenstein: 'Just a few weeks and the year 1943 would belong to the past. The war, with all its trials and tribulations, was going full blast. From North Cape to the Libyan Desert, and from Russia to the Atlantic, our forces were fighting. German ships were in action on practically all the seas and oceans. Since the entry of the United States into the war the Luftwaffe was inferior in numbers and the aircrews, continuously in action, were overstretched. The American airmen had things better. After happily surviving twenty five operations against the enemy, their war was over.

Prinz Wittgenstein, who was a *Jagdgruppen-kommandeur* in Schleswig, was given a new job. We were posted with our aircraft to Rechlin on the Müritzsee. A night fighting experimental unit was to be developed there. *Unteroffizier* Kurt Matzuleit, our flight engineer, and I were taken by surprise. In a few hours we were torn away from our circle of chums - in Rechlin we knew nobody and often sat around quite miserable. Prinz Wittgenstein was travelling most of the time for discussions of one kind or another, often to the *Reichsluftfahrtministerium* (Air Ministry) in Berlin.

For the most part our job was to keep the machine ready for action at all times. There were no night fighter units at Rechlin airfield. It often took me hours to collect

Feldwebel Friedrich Ostheimer, who flew with Wittgenstein during 16 of his 'kills' and survived the fatal crash of his Kommodore. Opposite - Ostheimer today.

by telephone all the operational documentation for wireless and navigation. As temporary accommodation a railway coach with sleeper compartments was placed at our disposal. During the time in Rechlin, about three weeks, we flew several operations over Berlin and I particularly remember two of these night operations.

In the flight control building Kurt and I had a small room at our disposal. When enemy incursions were reported we waited there for possible action. One evening it looked as if Berlin might be the target of the bomber stream. Prinz Wittgenstein had warned us that we should soon be taking off. So we flew off towards the south east, climbing in the direction of Berlin.

The distance from Rechlin to Berlin is about a hundred kilometres. The lady announcer on the Reich fighter wavelength gave continuous reports on the position, course and altitude of the enemy bombers. The latter were identified in the terminology by the code words, *"Dicke Autos"* (Big Cars). In this way, all fighters aloft were always accurately briefed on the situation in the air. Meanwhile Berlin had been identified as the target and the order came over the fighter wavelength: "All units to *Bär!*

All units to *Bär!*" In the meantime we had got to the same altitude as the bombers; it was about 7,000 metres. Flying on a south easterly course, we slotted into the bomber stream. The search radar was switched on and the airspace around us, so far as visibility permitted, was scanned.

I soon had my first target on the screen and gave the pilot the appropriate course corrections over the intercom. "Straight ahead, a bit higher." We very quickly reached the heavily laden four engined bomber, as nearly always it was a Lancaster. Prinz Heinrich set it alight with one burst of *Schräge Musik* and it went into a dive.

In front, the first searchlight fingers felt across the surface of the night sky. Anti-aircraft fire became more intense and, as a signal to begin, the British Pathfinder machines dropped their light cascades as orientation points for the approaching bombers. I already had another target on our radar screen, the distance to the enemy bomber quickly decreased. We could tell from the difference in speed alone that it had to be a bomber. Suddenly, however, the distance decreased, not just quickly but with a downright rush. I just had time to shout down the intercom: "Dive, dive, he's flying straight at us!" The bat of an eyelid later a shadow on a reciprocal course flashed over the top of us and away. We only felt the pressure of the air wave and the aircraft - presumably another Lancaster - disappeared into the darkness of the night. We three sat, as if paralysed, in our seats... The tension eased when Kurt said: "That was rather close!" Once again good fortune had smiled upon us.

On to the next target. The approach was almost completed, the pilot and the flight mechanic could already recognize the enemy machine. Then out of the blue the starboard engine started to vibrate, the propeller lost revolutions and finally stopped completely. Prinz Heinrich immediately put the machine's nose down to reduce speed, feathered the right hand propeller and altered the trim of the rudder against the good engine until a more or less normal flying attitude was achieved. By the time Wittgenstein had a grip on our machine, the Lancaster had long since escaped into the darkness.

Perhaps we could have achieved more success that night. However, with only one engine we had but one objective: back to Rechlin. I called up the D/F station by radio and asked for a course. The port engine was purring nicely and we flew slowly, losing height, tracking towards Rechlin. I also informed the D/F station that an engine had stopped and that we had to try and land on only one.

Every airman knows about the dangers and difficulties of such a landing in the dark. Actually we should have been frightfully scared again, but experience shows in such situations it does not help at all. Although it was in fact forbidden, Prinz Heinrich wanted to make a normal wheels down landing. That meant that if the approach was wrong it wouldn't be possible to overshoot with only one engine. It was a fair bet that machine and crew would be written off.

However Prinz Heinrich, as pilot and captain of our aircraft, was in command; the final decision was his. To help us get our bearings, bright flares, known to airmen as *"Radieschen"* (radishes) were fired over the airfield. When we had reached the airfield we first headed away from it and then flew in a wide arc to reach the approach path. The Prinz had to do it that way as the machine could only be turned about the engine which was still running. A turn about the engine which had stopped could easily have caused us to crash. We came into land using a VHF beacon, what was then a very precise landing aid. The one working engine was throttled back and at the same time the trim of the rudder had to be returned to normal. The landing was perfect, as the machine jolted along the runway a stone fell from our hearts. We were naturally full of praise for our pilot, and Kurt and I felt we had earned a short convalescence and a breather.

One of the last photographs. Christmas 1943
Wittgenstein as godfather to his nephew Alexander.

After a few days, the engine was changed and our machine was serviceable again. Prinz Wittgenstein was once more getting impatient. The next time the enemy bombers came over Berlin seemed to be the target again and we too were once more in the air. Exceptionally, the weather was good and at an average height there was a light stratum of mist; above that, it was cloudless. I switched my set to the *Reich* fighter wavelength and so on this occasion too we were again briefed on the general situation in the air. Everything pointed to an attack on the capital.

At this stage, large tracts of Berlin were heavily damaged. Whole streets lay in rubble, an unimaginable sight. I once experienced a night attack on the ground. With a crowd of other people I stood in an underground station; the earth shook with every bomb, women and children screamed, clouds of smoke rolled through the shafts. Anyone who did not experience fear and horror must have had a heart of stone.

Back to our operation. Between times we had reached the approach altitude of the bomber stream and, like the Lancasters, pressed on through the barrage of anti-aircraft fire over the city. British Pathfinder machines, which we called *"Zeremonienmeister"* (masters of ceremonies) had already dropped their flare cascades. Over the city was a picture which can hardly be described. All the searchlights were shining at the layer of mist hanging overhead and this looked like an illuminated pane of frosted glass, above which spread a great aura of light. Now you could see the attacking bombers, almost as if it were daylight. A unique sight!

Prinz Wittgenstein lightly nudged our Junkers to the side. We could see them flying, those who at other times were protected by the darkness of the night. At this moment we did not know where to attack first, but the decision was taken out of our hands. Tracers whizzed past us and unceremoniously jerked us out of our contemplation. *Major* Wittgenstein took the machine down in a steep curve. As we dived away I could still see the Lancaster flying obliquely over our heads with the gunner firing his twin guns at us from the mid upper turret. Fortunately he did not aim very well. It is true we had been hit a few times, but the engines maintained their revolutions and the crew were unhurt. We slipped off to the side into the darkness so that we could still just recognize the Lancaster.

We now flew on for a while parallel to the bomber cloaked in darkness. The darker it became around us, the closer we moved towards the enemy machine. As the illumination from the scarchlights became ever dimmer, and the fires started by the British attack lay behind us, we had well and truly crept up on the four-engined bomber. The Lancaster was now flying above us, suspecting nothing wrong. Perhaps the crew was already relieved by the thought that they had happily survived the attack and were now on the way home. However we, gripped by the excitement of the chase, sat tensely in our cabin, our gaze fixed rigidly upward. Hopefully they had not spotted us yet!

Prinz Wittgenstein brought our '88 even closer to the enormous shadow hanging over us, took careful aim and opened fire with the *Schräge Musik*. The trail of light from the 20 mm shells burned its way between the engines into a wing and set the fuel tanks alight. We swung immediately to the side and watched the burning Lancaster which continued on course for some distance. We were in no position to see whether the crew had succeeded in baling out. At all events there was sufficient time. In a bright flash of fire the bomber exploded, and blown into several pieces, fell to earth. At the same time I made good radio contact with our D/F station. We flew in the direction of Rechlin without any problems and landed there.

Radio communications between aircraft and ground station were very important, but they didn't always function as well as one might have wished. In this connection, I always remember a big attack on Hamburg. Despite bad weather, British bomber units flew towards the German North Sea coast. Because of rain and heavy clouds blowing up, we were not supposed to take off. In fact we were already in bed, however, when the incursions were reported we just had to take off. We were already drenched before we got to the machine and were sitting in the cabin. In the lightening flashes we saw the machines taxying for take-off. The cloud cover practically touched the ground, which virtually seemed to disappear as we took off. At about 6,500 metres we cleared the blanket of cloud. Because the atmosphere was electrically charged small flames formed at many points on our machine and on the propeller.[1] On the radio only the crackling of the electrical discharges could be heard.

In the area of Heligoland, our own anti-aircraft guns fired at us, not very welcome but at least we knew where we were! The British bombers suffered their first losses through icing up over the North Sea. We didn't make contact with the enemy that night. Due to the crackling on my set it was impossible to make contact with a D/F station. We hung around at an altitude of 7,000 metres over the North Sea and had neither radio contact, nor any ability to navigate. Our only chance was to fly south in the hope of finding an airfield in *Reich* territory or we would have to bail out. After countless efforts we then had a slight hope. When I turned the volume control of my receiver right down, I could faintly hear the radio beacon from Westerland airfield on the island of Sylt. With my D/F set I worked out the direction. We flew towards Westerland and landed there in poor visibility and after several dare-devil aerial manoeuvres.

A few days later we flew to Salzburg but returned to Rechlin again shortly before Christmas 1943. The originally planned night flying trials unit was, however, not set up. Wittgenstein was given a new job. He was appointed *Kommodore* of *2. Nachtjagdgeschwader*. On the last day, we packed our kit bags and flew to Arnheim-

---

[1] - *St Elmo's fire.*

Deelen in Holland. Here Kurt Matzuleit, the chief ground mechanic who had also flown with us, and I celebrated on New Year's Eve. The atmosphere was very depressed as we wondered what this war, which was becoming tougher and more horrible, might have in store for us in 1944. Millions of people who were all bound somehow in this frightful machinery of war will have had the same experience at the turn of the year.

20 JANUARY 1944

Friedrich Ostheimer continues his story: 'On the afternoon of 20 January Kurt Matzuleit and I went to the dispersal point where our Junkers 88 stood. We were responsible for the aircraft's serviceability. Kurt's job was to inspect the two engines; nowadays one would call it a 'check-up'. Kurt ran the engines on high revolutions, the rev count, oil and fuel pressure were checked. A check of the petrol tanks was part of the process, they had to be filled right to the top, that and thousands of other things. It was my job to check the radio and navigation equipment; naturally I had to be sure that the radar was functioning. The whole installation consisted of a long, medium and short wave transmitter, as well as a VHF and D/F set and a radar with which I could locate the enemy aircraft. It was not possible to repair the installations in flight, the most I could do was to change a fuse.

For whatever reason, we were not accommodated with the rest of the night fighter crews. The result was that every day I had to worry about the night's weather forecast, and also fetch the radio and navigation documentation. The weather forecasts for the night from 20 to 21 January 1944 were not good. Over England there was so called *Rückseitenwetter* (cold sector weather), that meant broken cloud and good visibility. Over Holland and Germany, on the other hand, air activity was considerably impeded by a bad weather front, with a very low cloud ceiling and mediocre visibility. It was ideal attacking weather for the British bomber formations. For some time the Royal Air Force had had the so-called *'Rotterdam'* (H2S) set, a device the radio beams of which were aimed at the ground and which made the terrain they were overflying visible on a screen. The Pathfinder machines again flew ahead of the bomber stream and were able to pick out on the *'Rotterdam'* the target for attack and then mark it with flare cascades. The worse the weather conditions were for us, the better they were for the attacker. That was precisely the kind of night on which one had to reckon with an attack.

We three, the senior NCO of the ground crew, the flight engineer and I were waiting in a small hut near the hangar, right next to the runway. Outside it was raining; it was after all January and correspondingly cold. Inside, it was pleasant and comfortably warm. In such a situation it was best not think at all about a possible order to take off. Over in the hangar stood our Ju 88. The tanks were filled with 3,500 litres of aviation spirit and all weapons fully armed. Two BMW radial engines supplied the power for a high flying speed, aided by the fact that on our machine the fuselage, wings and rudder were finely rubbed down and polished.

The night was not yet very old when a huge radar, the so-called *Wassermann* equipment, picked up the first enemy aircraft. The installation was located on a North Sea island. Soon after this the *Gefechtsstand* (Command Post) issued the provisional order, *"Sitzbereitschaft"* (cockpit readiness). Matzuleit went to the machine at once, our senior ground crew NCO waited by the telephone, but soon came running after us.

Prinz Wittgenstein, our pilot and, at the same time, *Kommodore* of *Nachtjagdgeschwader* 2, usually waited in the *Gefechtsstand* to keep up to date with the air situation. From there he told us we should soon be taking off. We plugged in our starter which helped to turn the engines and the machine was rolled out of the hangar. In the meantime, I had already switched on my radio receiver and could hear the messages from the *Gefechtsstand*. There, the D/F locations of the enemy bombers were noted by *Luftwaffe* female signals assistants on a large, indirectly illuminated frosted glass screen.

As soon as it was clear that the first British machines had taken off and were flying over the English coast to the North Sea, Prinz Wittgenstein could not stay in his chair. He raced across the runway in his car, stopped by the machine, was helped into his flying suit and climbed through the trap into the aircraft. His first order: "Ostheimer, transmit we are taking off at once!" I reported take-off with our call sign R4-XM. The trap door was shut.

Examining a chart. In the background a
basket of flowers, the dedication card read:

'To their famous night fighter from the grateful population.'

Laurels for Prinz Wittgenstein

We taxied to the start point and as soon as the runway controller gave us the green light, the engines gave a roar.

We rushed along the thin line of runway lamps and seconds later were swallowed up by the dark of the night. Climbing, we set course for Heligoland. Somewhere, out over the North Sea, we were bound to cross the approach course of the enemy bombers. All round us was the pitch-black night. Only the phosphorescent luminosity of the instruments was to be seen. Flame dampers were fitted to the engines in order to remain as invisible as possible to the enemy. In this situation flying was solely on instruments and the only link with the earth were the messages from the *Gefechtsstand* at Arnheim-Deelen. In this way we were continually briefed about the position, course and altitude of the enemy formation. We determined our own position by VHF Direction Finding. I could pass data to the pilot via the intercom and, if the situation required, he could change course. The further we advanced over the North Sea, the better the weather. Now the cloud was no longer quite closed in. Overhead a few stars twinkled individually, and thousands of metres below, we could recognize the surface of the North Sea. It made me shudder to think it might be necessary to fight to survive in that cold water. Fortunately the flight left little time to pursue such gloomy broodings.

In the meantime we had reached an altitude of 7,000 metres and must actually be very close to the bomber stream. I pressed in the high voltage switch on the visual display, opened a flap at my feet and pulled up the equipment with the monitor. As we were already at a great height I could use the equipment to pick targets at distances up to seven kilometres, but there was still nothing to be seen.

Suddenly, however, the first searchlights appeared in front of us and to the right. They were feeling the night sky with their fingers of light. Meanwhile you could see the flashes of exploding anti-aircraft shells. Now we knew the whereabouts of the bomber stream. *Major* Wittgenstein pushed the throttles lightly and we made a fast beeline for our target. It was clear to us that things were about to get serious. The tension rose, the excitement of the chase made the pulse beat faster. On my search radar the screen flickered, uncertainly at first, but then I spotted a target. I naturally told the *Major* immediately and gave him the position and range. Just a small correction and we had the target exactly six kilometres in front of us. I activated a particular lever on the radar. There was a vertical line on the screen which could be brought across to meet the horizontal line. This enabled me to establish whether the bomber was higher or lower than we were. As usual we flew towards the target at a slightly higher altitude. The bomber's range decreased by the second, the tension in the cabin rose and rose.

My heart was in my mouth, my hands were ice cold and wet with sweat. Only a thousand metres still separated us from our target, a British bomber. The conversation in the cabin became, involuntarily, ever quieter, even though the enemy obviously could not hear us. The British airmen certainly had no inkling, as yet, of the danger threatening them. Then the image of the enemy bomber disappeared from the screen in its own reflection. Seconds later we were underneath the enemy machine. It was a Lancaster, like an enormous cruciform shadow hovering over us. Four engines, wide spread wings, a box-shaped fuselage, twin fins and, at the tail, a gun turret with quadruple machine guns; where it hits, the shreds fly. Our nerves were stretched to breaking point. The flight engineer had loaded the guns, the reflex sight on the cabin roof was switched on, and our speed matched to that of the Lancaster. The bomber flew 50 to 60 metres above us. It was an almost peaceful picture; just as if nobody knew anything about death and war; just as if the enemy was not dragging a fuselage filled with destructive bombs; just as if the British had never heard anything about German night fighters.

All that was to change in a split second; Prinz Wittgenstein had the bomber's wing in our sights. I also stared upward, as if mesmerised. Very gently the pilot nudged our machine to the right, trained the sight just in front of the wing between the two engines and pressed the button. A blazing tongue of fire roared towards the bomber. Immediately a chain of explosions tore open the wing and fuel tanks, the bomber's wing burned furiously. In the initial shock the British pilot pulled the bomber up over the right wing and we had to turn away at high speed in order to avoid the area of the fire. Fascinated, we watched for a moment as the bomber, shrouded in flames, dived like a comet in a broad curve to earth. Prinz Wittgenstein, an outstanding shot, had fired with the *Schräge Musik* and scored a direct hit with the 20 mm cannons which were almost vertical.

After a few minutes, Matzuleit reported the crash and the time, we could only hope the Lancaster had not crashed in an inhabited area, unable as we were to establish this from our position; at the moment the bomber caught fire, we made a quick getaway. After all, there were more bombers still in the air and there were possibly long range night fighters, who might have caught sight of us in the glare of the burning bomber. A bit outside the bomber stream we calmed ourselves down for a few minutes before starting off for the next attack. Here and there we could see burning aircraft diving into the night; so our fighters were having some success.

Directly after that, the order came over the Reich fighter wavelength: *"Alles nach Bär!"* (All units to Bär!) That meant Berlin had been identified as the target, so all available fighters began to track in the direction of Berlin. We were soon making our next approach as we quickly picked up another target on our screen. No wonder, there were several hundred enemy bombers in the air! In between times the British airmen had already noticed what was going on and were using all kinds of tricks to make our life more difficult and shake us off. They did not want to be an easy target for the fighters and constantly changed their course and speed. However that did not do much good since I soon had two targets on the screen. We took the nearer one. Everything went the same way as our first approach but, because of the restless behaviour of the enemy and his constant change of position, we had a more difficult time. For safety's sake we made our approach at a lower altitude, in order to avoid coming suddenly into the range of the rear gunner's quadruple machine guns. When we got under the Lancaster again we could see, in the weak starlight, the four barrels pointing out of the rear turret.

Just as during the first attack of the night, the tension in the cabin was at breaking point. Carefully, Prinz Wittgenstein moved closer to the Lancaster and, this time too, fired the *Schräge Musik*. Immediately after the first burst the Lancaster was alight. She flew on course for a moment longer but then slipped to the side and dived into the depths. After a while, Matzuleit again reported the impact and explosion. Whether any of the British airmen was able to escape by parachute we could not tell. However, the chances were good since we did not fire at the fuselage and cabin. This time too we got out of the way of the diving aircraft, at high speed.

At short intervals we saw a number of other machines dropping in flames. It was a gruesome business. But we had no time to ponder, because I already had the next aircraft on my screen, almost as a matter of routine we flew up to the target. Prinz Wittgenstein came pretty close to the Lancaster which was being flown very erratically. On this occasion too, a burst from *Schräge Musik* blew a big hole in the wing and started a blazing fire. This time the British pilot reacted unusually, he remained at the controls of his burning machine and dived down on top of us. Our Prinz too, whipped the Ju 88 into a dive, but the blazing monster came closer and closer and hung in visual contact over our cabin. I had only one thought: "We've had it!!!" A heavy blow staggered our aircraft, Prinz Wittgenstein lost control of the machine and we went into a spin, plunging down into the night. If we had not been strapped in, we would certainly have been catapulted out of the cabin. After a dive of about 3,000 metres, Wittgenstein was able to bring the machine under control and onto an even keel.

As surveyed as best we could in the dark, everything on our machine seemed to be in order, but where we were at that moment nobody had a clue beyond a rough guess that it was between the west and south west of Berlin. Now I became the most important man on board. I tried first of all to contact several airfields in the area where we presumably were by Morse on medium wave, but I got no answer. Prinz Wittgenstein was already slightly cross. From my radio handbook, I found the wavelength of *"Flugsicherungshauptstelle, Köln"* (Flight Safety HQ in Cologne). I made contact quickly and got the required fix on my position. Saalfeld was the answer, about 100 kilometres south-west of Leipzig. I asked for the nearest airfield open for night landing and quickly switched to the appropriate frequency and signalled SOS, aircraft in trouble. The RDF station at Erfurt-Bindersleben acknowledged promptly and gave me an approach course.

The weather was again as bad as it could be, we slowly lost height and dipped into the clouds. Further D/F's brought us nearer to the airfield. From the RDF station I also heard the local weather report: Cloud base 300 metres. That should be good enough for a landing. "Aircraft over airfield," said the RDF station. We turned off into the direction given, slowly lost more height and, after a 225 degree turn, were making our landing approach. We had broken through the cloud and saw the airfield landing lights in front of us. I continued calling up for bearings throughout the approach. We were well on course, the undercarriage and flaps were down, the height reduced and the engines throttled back further.

At this moment the machine began, for no obvious reason, to dip to the right. Prinz Wittgenstein increased engine speed and the aircraft levelled up. The wing had obviously been damaged by the burning bomber. At a height of about 800 metres, we simulated a landing approach. It was the same again. As soon as the engine speed dropped, the machine dropped its right wing dangerously. Naturally, in the darkness, we could not see how serious the damage was. Now there were two ways of getting down in one piece in a situation like this, either we jumped by parachute or we made a wheels up landing at higher speed. We decided on the second option, which was not quite without risk, and I radioed our decision to the D/F station. We did a few more circuits to allow time for the fire and ambulance crews to take up position and then came in to land. I felt for the handle to jettison the cabin roof and gripped it with both hands. The landing flaps were lowered again and the engines only slightly throttled back.

As the lights at the edge of the airfield flashed by underneath, I ripped the handle backwards. The slipstream tore the cabin roof from the fuselage with a noise like an explosion. Moments later a heavy blow; *Major* Wittgenstein had set the machine down on the grass beside the runway and the machine shot forward on the rain-soaked ground. It tore the floor plating away beneath us and chopped-up tufts of grass whizzed through the cabin. After one or two hard thumps the machine stopped and I released my safety belt with a jerk and banged the parachute harness release. Jumping over the wing onto the grass I threw myself to the ground and lay there because the machine might also have exploded. The fire tender and ambulances roared up but we'd had tremendous luck and nobody was hurt. With the help of a searchlight we could, at last, inspect the damage. In the collision the Lancaster had torn off two metres off the right wing and with one of the four propellers the Englishman had chopped a big hole in the fuselage about a metre behind the cabin. We could thank our lucky stars to have survived this collision. There was great relief all round! We had landed safely in Erfurt-Bindersleben or, more accurately, had put our machine down on its belly. In the mess we got something to eat and, after that, even a good bed to sleep in.

On the following day we flew back to Deelen in the Netherlands in another machine. Kurt Matzuleit, our flight engineer, and I should have much preferred to travel back in the comfort of a train. For us it would have been a relaxation we had earned and, on such a trip, we should have been able to distance ourselves from the terrors of the previous night. But there was no peace. Prinz Wittgenstein had almost got to the top among the night fighters, and that drove him on to achieve even more; thus we had landed back in Deelen before lunch. Kurt and I wanted to take our ease and, for once, not think about operations and shooting down, but it was to turn out quite differently.'

21 JANUARY 1944

'Scarcely an hour had passed after lunch and we had just arrived at our billet when we were startled by the telephone. I picked up the receiver. The caller was Prinz Wittgenstein. He said: "We are flying in *Oberleutnant* so and so's machine today (I have forgotten the name). Go to the dispersal point with Matzuleit and make sure the machine is ready for take-off by tonight." The only answer I had was, *"Jawohl, Herr Major!"* Secretly we had hoped that for a couple of days, or at least until the arrival of a replacement aircraft, we should not have to think of death, war and disaster.

After a short rest we went off to the dispersal point. As usual, Kurt went over the engines and ran them up checking the rev count, oil pressure, fuel pressures and function of the magnetos. The tanks had to be full to the brim, the weapons checked and replacement ammunition stowed. I checked the whole radio installation and the radar sets, in so far as this was possible on the ground. Finally the machine was reported to the *Kommodore* as being ready for action. That evening we three sat in the small hut near the hangar and waited to see what was going to happen. Outside it was raining and it was cold, just the kind of weather when you would not have put a dog outside. We were beginning to think the Tommies'd had a bellyful and had preferred to stay in the warm. I had lain down, still dressed in full flying gear, on a bunk in a next door room. I was thinking how, a few days before, the Prinz - our pilot - had invited *Unteroffizier* Matzuleit, the senior NCO of our ground crew, and me to dinner. Wittgenstein had shot a wild sheep in the large game park directly adjoining the Deelen airfield. There was roast liver and wine.

I was tired and, to start with, fell asleep immediately, but then I woke up and could not get to sleep again. All sorts of thoughts wandered through my head. Mostly they were thoughts about chums with whom we'd been sitting

Schmid, Kommandierender General des XII. Fliegerkorps. Wittgenstein's last superior.

at readiness a few days ago and who, after a night operation, are "missing in action." They will probably never be among us again. That brought melancholy and a measure of hopelessness into the heart. Boundless uncertainty lay like a great weight on the chest and made the bitterness of those days even bleaker. You were gripped by anxiety, like a polyp's arms, when you thought of the night and all the dangers associated with it.

I wondered whether this grisly war would ever come to an end. Again and again I put these thoughts to the back of my mind. We gritted our teeth, started up our engines and, through the darkness rain and fog, threw ourselves against the enemy bombers - "come hell or high water." We fighting men in this war had the duty to protect the women and children at home. Often this thought overcame fear.

Matzuleit snatched me none too gently from my reverie with him calling, *"Sitzbereitschaft!"* I stood up at once, shaking the sleep from my body and the thoughts out of my head. I took my navigator's bag and ran to the aircraft; from experience I knew Prinz Wittgenstein was always in a particular hurry to get into the air. I remember the night of 1/2 January 1944, on that occasion I reported the first "kill" even before all the aircraft of our *Gruppe* had time to take off. Today too, I had the radio working and was listening to the voice of a woman *Luftwaffe* auxiliary in the *Gefechtsstand* as Prinz Heinrich was climbing into the cabin. *"Alles in Ordnung?"* was his first question, *"Jawohl, Herr Major!"* my answer. Matzuleit climbed in immediately afterwards and the ground crew's number one shut the trap door from the outside. Now we only had to put our helmets on, place throat microphones in position and put the oxygen mask on. High altitude would require this soon but we started on the ground because we had found it enhanced our night vision. We taxied to the start line, the engines roared and after a short run the machine rose into its element.

We did not care to think about the dangers which awaited us outside in the dark. Climbing again, in a north-easterly direction towards the North Sea. Over the sea were the bombers carrying death and destruction, flying towards the German coast. According to reports from Ground Control, the bomber stream was flying at 8,000 metres. The first anti-aircraft fire could be seen, so the bombers could not be very far away. In the meantime, we had reached the same altitude as the enemy aircraft. Like a signal to attack, an aircraft burst into flames in front of us and went down like a burning torch. Now our pilot made a right turn on to the same course as the bombers. The hunt in the dark began again.

For some time we had been not only hunters but also the hunted. Ever more British long range night fighters accompanied the bombers to hold losses within limits. On my radar the first target showed up. After a small course correction we had it right in front of us, flying rather higher than our machine. The distance shrank visibly, so it was most likely a bomber. The previous night's collision was fresh in our minds, so we made our approach at a rather lower altitude. As the shadow of the enemy aircraft pushed slowly over us, it could be recognized as a Lancaster against the starry sky. After only one burst from the *Schräge Musik*, the left wing was immediately in flames. The burning Lancaster went down into a shallow dive, which then turned into a spin. With an enormous explosion the fully laden bomber crashed, its lethal cargo exploding with it. It was between 2200 and 2205 hours.

We went on searching and at times I had up to six different targets on my radar screen. We had quickly carried out two small course corrections and already had the next target in front of us, another Lancaster. A burst of fire and, to start with, the aircraft burned a little, then dived steeply over the left wing. Shortly after that, I saw the fire as it crashed. It was about 2020 hours.

A few seconds after the actual crash there was a series of very violent explosions, presumably the bombs. After a short run up another target had been found and knocked down with a heavy burst. I don't know precisely when, but it must have been around 2230 when I noted the crash. Then everything went very fast indeed. A few minutes later we had another four-engined bomber in our sights. Like a pike in a lake full of carp we were now flying in the middle of the bomber stream. Our situation was not without danger but in our euphoria we didn't think about it.

This enemy bomber too went down in flames after the first attack. It was meanwhile 2240 hours when I observed the crash. This time too is only approximate, because all the notes I made during the flight went missing when we had to bale out. I already had the next targets on the radar screen. After two slight course corrections we had another Lancaster in front of us. After a single attack the fuselage was alight, but the fire became smaller and smaller and we approached for another attack. We were soon in position and Major Wittgenstein was about to shoot when there was banging and flashing in our machine. The left wing immediately caught fire and the aircraft began to dive.

Then I saw the cabin roof above our heads fly away and a shout on the intercom which sounded like *"Raus!"* (Out!). I tore my oxygen mask and helmet off and was catapulted out of the machine. After a while I pulled the parachute release and landed about 15 minutes afterwards to the east of the Hohengöhrener Damm, near Schönhausen (not far from Rathenow). Insofar as I could reconstruct what happened at all, we had been fired at from below. I could not observe much more than that.'

Two days later, on 23 January 1944, Ostheimer had

to write a so-called *Luftkampfzeugenbericht* (Air Combat Witness Report). His official report partially confirms verbatim what he recalls today.

Ostheimer's account continues: 'We were thrown out of the cabin by the explosion of the wing. Once it was possible for me to grasp a clear thought again, the machine had disappeared. I spun around in the air from about 8,000 metres down to 7,500 metres. By stretching out my arms and legs, the twirling gradually died down. Way below me, the cloud lay like a winter landscape. The parachute which was still closed gave me a reassuring feeling.

We had fortunately learned that it was a mistake to open the parachute at heights above 5,000 metres because it would have caused a disastrous shortage of oxygen. While I was rushing down, I kept hearing the drone of flying aircraft nearby. My greatest concern was being hit. I began to count slowly from 20 to 60, that's what we had been taught. Then I waited a while longer before opening the parachute. A hard jerk and I hung in the shrouds. One fear less.

I looked around but could not see another parachute. Where could Prinz Wittgenstein and Matzuleit be? Now, for the first time I noticed that the fur boot was missing from my right leg. I pulled my right leg up as far as I could in the circumstances, opened the zip on the left boot, and pushed the right foot inside. Slowly, I came closer to the cloud cover and wondered what the ground underneath would look like, then the clouds swallowed me up. It became darker all round me and visibility was virtually non existent. This situation lasted quite a while until I could suddenly see the ground beneath me. Forest with white patches of snow in between. To get my bearings, I shot off a signal flare.

At this point I had just one more anxiety, to survive. By mistake, I had shot off a flare with a small parachute which now drifted towards me, but fortunately did not set light to my parachute. I had just replaced the flare pistol in my flying overall when there was a rustle and I lay on the ground between the trees in a clearing. My watch showed 2320 hours.

I bundled up the parachute, sat down on it and

considered what to do next. There was no sense in sitting and waiting, it was too cold for that. I rolled up the parachute and carried it on my back, if necessary I could wrap myself in it if I found no shelter. I suddenly felt an excruciating pain in my right ankle joint, and did not know how much further I should be able to walk on it. After a time, I came to a track and in the light of my flash lamp I could see the wheel marks of a car and the imprint of horses' hooves. I went in the direction taken by the car.

The pains in my right foot became increasingly fiercer and I had to rest more frequently and warm the foot. I had been walking through the wood for around two hours when I saw the outline of a roof in front of me. I shot off a flare and saw several houses standing between the trees. Then I heard voices in front of me and began to get a bit nervous. I shone my flashlamp at myself and called, *"Deutscher Flieger, nicht schießen!"* (German flyer, don't shoot). There was a good reason for doing this, since I knew the story of a *Staffel* chum who fell into a front garden in the Hanover area. He was beaten up by the outraged people who thought him to be British.

The people had already seen me sailing down by parachute and now took me into their house. I was glad of a chance to sit down at last and to put my painful foot up. I was also fed very well. I reported by telephone to the airfield at Stendal and an ambulance came to collect me.

Flight engineer Kurt Matzuleit also came down by parachute. I met up with him again at Deelen a few days later. He survived the war, but I have lost track of him.'

Ostheimer concluded his eyewitness report with the following observation: 'Very early the next morning, Prinz Wittgenstein was found near the crash site. It seems he hit his head on the tail fin or plane, was knocked unconscious and could not pull the rip-cord of his parachute.

Around the time of 21 January 1944 the area round Schönhausen/Elbe was not regarded as a theatre of operations, so Wittgenstein could not be buried there with other war dead. He was lying in a closed coffin on Stendal airfield. I lay in the sick bay with a cracked ankle joint, but could get around on crutches so in this way got to the place where the coffin was located.'

A witness living in the area gives the following account of the Prinz's last moments: 'Wittgenstein's aircraft was badly damaged by a long range British night fighter. The gunner and wireless operator both baled out. It looked as if the pilot had tried to fly the aircraft to Stendal-Borstel airfield which was often used for refuelling, or emergency landings of German night fighters. After ten or twelve kilometres when he was steadily losing height, he touched the ground in the Lübers district, between Hohengöhren and Klietz, shot over meadows and arable land and lost his undercarriage when he dipped into a forest plantation. The wreckage of the Ju 88 was then found spread over a wide area. About two hundred metres from the place where the fuselage burnt out, the doctor of the nearby arms factory, Deutsche Sprengchemie Klietz, Dr Gerhard Kaiser, found the body of the Prinz early in the morning of 22 January 1944. A farmer telephoned the doctor very early and told him an aircraft had crashed in the neighbourhood during the night. It was said the coffin was later taken to Holland.'

After the war, the doctor became Director of the Orthopaedic Clinic and Polyclinic at Humboldt University in (East) Berlin. Having meanwhile reached the age of 80, the doctor wrote on 20 July 1990 from memory: 'So far as I remember, I was telephoned between five and six in the morning. I got up at once, got dressed and drove off. I did not see the aircraft itself. Lots of pieces were scattered over a large area. I had to search for about a half an hour before I found the Prinz's body. The dead man lay in the wood, west of the Hohengöhren-Klietz road, and was not mutilated. Rigor mortis had set in; on the face there were large cyanosed patches but no serious injuries. I saw no bullet wound or blood. We civilians were only allowed to examine military personnel if they showed signs of life. In this case the onset of rigor mortis confirmed that he had died several hours before. For this reason I did not open the uniform and laid the dead man back as I had found him. It was now a job for the *Wehrmacht* pathologist to reconstruct the crash and the death of the Prinz. In my view, the Prinz was thrown out of the aircraft. However, I did not see the remains of a parachute. I drove straight to

Totenschein

1. Name und Vorname: (Bei Totgeborenen Name des Vaters, bei unehelichen Totgeborenen Name der Mutter)	Prinz zu Sayn Wittgenstein Heinrich
2. Beruf, Stand, Geschäft: (Bei Kindern Beruf usw. der Eltern)	Aktiver Offizier (Major)
3. Sterbeort: (Straße und Hausnummer)	Lübars-Schönhauser-Damm (Krs. Stendal)
4. Geboren:	den 14.8.1916 Kopenhagen
5. Gestorben: (Totgeboren)	den 21. Januar 19 44 gegen ~~nachts~~ 23 Uhr
6. Todesursache: (Möglichst genau angeben!) a) Grundleiden? b) Begleitkrankheiten? c) Nachfolgende Krankheiten? d) Welches der vorgenannten Leiden hat den Tod unmittelbar herbeigeführt? (Bei gewaltsamen Sterbefällen — Selbstmord, Mord, Totschlag, Verunglückung — sind besondere, genaue Einzelangaben erforderlich)	Feindeinwirkung(Flugzeugabschuss) ———————— ———————— ———————— Geschlossener Bruch des Gehirn-und Gesichtschädels
7. Ärztlich behandelt?	nein

(Ort) Stendal den 24. 1. 19 44

(Arzt) J. Peter

Stabsarzt u. Führer der Lw.San.-Staffel.

Vordruck 1207
Verlag: Dansa'sche Buchdruckerei

154

the police in Klietz and reported the event. As I was told later, the soldiers were then quickly on the scene. On the afternoon of the second day, the Swedish Ambassador from Berlin came to see me. He said he was a friend of the Wittgenstein family and asked me for an account which he promised to pass on.'

The death certificate was issued by *Stabsarzt* Dr Peter, commanding officer of the *Luftwaffe Sanitäts-Staffel* and gives the cause of death as, "simple fractures of the skull in the area of the crown and face."

Hitler and Göring condoled, the *Wehrmacht communiqué* reported the loss and the Prinz was posthumously awarded the Oak Leaves with Swords to the Iron Cross. On 29 January 1944 the funeral took place at the Military Cemetery at Deelen. In 1948, when a general re-interment took place, the Prinz's remains were transferred to Ijsselstein (Netherlands), where Prinz Heinrich zu Sayn-Wittgenstein has since rested among 30,000 other German soldiers.

The German poetess, Ricarda Huch published the following poem to mark his death:

To a Hero

You who battled and prevailed,
Loosen the bronze plate on your breast;
May the starlight you escaped,
Flow cool around your still heart.

The heavy corn, the drunken grape,
You passed in breathless battle!
Oh Hero, may the cathedral of night,
Cover your slumber with fragrant clouds.

No homeland bells on doves' wings
To tell you evening's come,
You had instead of victory, triumph and spoils
A dark wreath and deep, deepest rest.

You who wrestled till the end
Will wake one day to the trumpet's call,
and begirt with the sword,
Turn your visage proudly into the redness of morn.

The commanding officer of *Luftflotte 5, General* Kammhuber, wrote of him: 'The night fighters have lost their best. It seems to be the unalterable will of fate that the very best, Richthofen, Mölders and Wittgenstein should be killed in the full bloom of their youth. The only comfort is in the knowledge of their heroism and immortality.'

January 1944. The funeral.

Wittgenstein's Commanding General made the following speech to the assembled personnel after Heinrich's death: 'Comrades, I see the unforgettable Major Prinz zu Sayn-Wittgenstein before me. He often came to me; he always had a hundred ideas, suggestions, opinions on how to make our performance in the great battle more effective and to protect the *Reich*. But on the margin of service matters, there spoke from the short sentences, and almost shy hints, a rich young heart, full of longing for a beautiful and uncomplicated life, some time, when the great peace had been won. He was an example to us all.'

A few personal traits may serve to further

understanding of this unique soldier's nature. Even in his boyhood a strong ascetic trait developed in him, a contempt for all the comforts of life, a real passion for the hardest feats which he wrung from his delicate frame. At this time a powerful love of Germany developed, coupled with a burning resentment of the *Versailles Diktat* (see endnote). From this time onwards his life was purposefully directed at toughening himself up. It was self evident to him that, although an expatriate German, he should join the Hitler Youth and convey his glowing idealism to his subordinates. When he became acquainted with flying there was nothing else in the world he wanted to do. His whole being belonged to his beloved *Luftwaffe*. Always taciturn and serious, he became more and more quiet, almost ascetic. Because of this his rare and shy, almost ironic, smile gave even more pleasure and one was pleased on the rare occasion when he something to say for himself. There was nothing he hated more than to be regarded as a hero and object of admiration.

He said: 'Night fighting is the most difficult but also the highest level of flying in existence. It is lucky that I always see the enemy before he sees me.' He shot quickly and in a masterly fashion, and went right close up in order to hit the enemy's most vulnerable point. He was an inexhaustible producer of, in part, trail-blazing technical and tactical ideas. This is the reason why, in 18 months of night fighting, he quickly overtook many colleagues in the numbers of enemy aircraft shot down. As early as August 1943, he moved up to the leading group with 64 night victories.

At that time, on his 27th birthday, the head of his family gave him the beautiful presentation sabre which had belonged to his famous forebear, the Russian Imperial Field Marshal Ludwig Adolf Peter zu Sayn-Wittgenstein, to whom it was presented in commemoration of his victory over Napoleon's Grande Armée. The young holder of the Oak Leaves was surely worthy of it.

At the beginning of January 1944, after just two years as a night fighter, he reached 72 'kills' and took the lead over his peers, keeping it until his death. Even on the night of 20 January 1944 he miraculously escaped death for the last time when, having shot down three bombers, he was rammed by a fourth such giant machine.

It was a tremendous feat of airmanship to make, as he did, an emergency landing with his badly damaged aircraft. On the following day, the other duties of a *Kommodore* deprived him of the rest he so badly needed. However when renewed enemy incursions were reported that night, there was no stopping him and, in spite of all the strain he climbed into the pilot's seat again. All the same the exhausted *Kommodore* shot down five of the juggernauts down and increased his score of 'kills' to 83. Unexpectedly he took extremely heavy fire from behind and to the side. His machine burst into flames and had to be abandoned. The last man to bail out saw Wittgenstein still at the controls. How he met his death remains obscure.

You can interpret it as you will. However the present day reader certainly has the critical distance to understand the following.

An excerpt from the official announcement by Göring the Commander in Chief of the *Luftwaffe*: 'The German *Luftwaffe* mourns the death of one of its most successful night fighters and unit leaders, who seemed to be assured of a brilliant future. The German people, who owe the men of the night fighters a profound debt of gratitude, stand with us in deep grief at the bier of the young hero. Inspired by an uncommon attacking spirit he had, in a short time, earned himself an undying fame. He crowned his heroic courage with the highest sacrifice of the soldier. For us, his death is a symbol of the pitiless and unsparing defensive battle we are fighting against the enemy terror formations. The *Geschwader*, which Major Prinz zu Sayn-Wittgenstein led in nightly battle against the enemy, will fight on in the spirit of their absolutely fearless young *Kommodore*, just as we all shall wish to see the exhortation and commitment implicit in his death.'

As stated, a kind of contemporary document which simply belongs in this memorial volume.

However then was not only the time for emotive obituaries of an official kind, poems were also written. We have already read one by Ricarda Huch. Ernst Mees, a *Leutnant* and pilot in Wittgenstein's *Nachtgeschwader*, whose account of the Prinz we have likewise read, also composed four stanzas after Heinrich's death. He simply headed his verses 'For Heinrich Prinz zu Wittgenstein.'

A narrow mean grave, the ropes slide
Heavy and heavier through friends' hands.
In time with the salvoes eternities fall -
As he sinks down silently, whom they knew.

A cool breath touches the faces,
As the cloak of death rustles through the ranks
They stand rigid, look into the lights of the bright day -
Will it be the same for me?

They feel not the cloak which brushed them,
they think, he was so young and joyful,
now he is a stranger, early mature yet near us
and yet already somewhere else.

They see him smile - their senses empathize
in distance, where the Great Godhead listens.
Then they fly. And free airs wash
around their forehead, they do not feel the cool
the dark death, which surrounds them.

Finally we should quote the poem written by Heinrich's mother, Prinzessin Walburga, after the death of her son:

You wore a secret crown -
the ways to you were far.
You lived in night and stars
in darkest silence.

You hunted - an eagle in the sky
You had an imperious blood -
And knew only flying and conquering
And the heat of serious battle.

For below in darkening latitudes
Lay your beloved land.
The oath of loyalty unto death
was burned into your heart.

Thus was your proud death
To us both sorrow and pride.
With a sword in my heart I say:
You were my son.

Fritz Bode, a citizen of Bendorf-Sayn, Wittgenstein's ancestral home district, wrote in a reader's letter of 1946:

'The millions of dead must not be forgotten. One should remind oneself of their greatness and tragedy through the brave Heinrich Prinz zu Sayn-Wittgenstein who represents many.'

The German Military Cemetery at Ijsselstein in Northern Holland
Thirty-thousand German soldiers, among them
Prinz Wittgenstein, are buried here.

Versailles Diktat - Properly *'Versailler Vertrag'* - 'Treaty of Versailles' the Germans commonly used *'Diktat'* to suggest that the treaty was imposed, rather than negotiated.

EPILOGUE

Then, as now, we honour the man who lays down his life for others, whether he is a stretcher bearer who brings a wounded man out of the front line, or the miner who rescues someone who is buried, or the night fighter who defends the homeland. They are all heroes and examples whom we need no less today. Wittgenstein was one of them - hence this book.

ADDENDUM

The following documents can be regarded as a supplement.

The miltary situation at the time of Wittgenstein's death is mentioned as the background for the direction of air warfare against the civilian population. Personal thoughts and experiences of people who witnessed at first hand the bombing of Coventry and Dresden are quoted in the hope they will carry with them some of the horror of this diabolical turn in modern warfare. These are followed by observations about Bomber Command, brought up to date by the dedication of a statue to Air Marshal Harris in London.

Finally, the Author takes over again with:

'The Vision'

As a friend of Prinz Wittgenstein and familiar with his way of thinking, and also as an operational pilot during the war, the Author's attempts to portray the thoughts and feelings of Prinz Wittgenstein as he might have, or did, experience them during the last moments of his life.

THE MILITARY SITUATION

BEGINNING OF 1944

Stalingrad and El Alamein had fallen. The Red Army had crossed the Polish-Soviet border, Leningrad had been relieved, the counter-offensive at Kursk had begun, Orel had been captured and the Ukraine and Kuban bridgeheads retaken. The partisan war behind the German lines was escalating. In the East peace reigned before the storm.

The unrestricted U-Boat war, which reached its peak in the convoy battles of 1943, had to suffer painful losses of its own, the successes declined and the battleship Scharnhorst was lost.

In September 1943, the US Armed Forces landed at Salerno in considerable numbers. Badoglio changed sides. The threatened Invasion, decided by Roosevelt, Churchill and Stalin tied down German forces on the Atlantic Wall.

Bomber Command's bad weather night attacks on German towns had increased. The British disrupted the German radar defences by dropping clouds of aluminium strips. The Americans had gone over to mass attacks in daylight. The material superiority of the Allies had begun to exert pressure. Since November the RAF had been bombing Berlin. Their average losses had sunk to 2% per operation; our own losses, due mostly to weather conditions, rose to 3%. Fighters had to be withdrawn from both Western and Eastern Fronts for air defence over German territory.

The battered German aircraft industry had increasing difficulty in the short term delivery of newly developed types ready for mass production. In addition there were problems with engines. So the strength of units fell to a fraction of their establishment. The factories producing equipment for the *Luftwaffe* were incapable of building the required numbers of bombers and fighters at the same time, so priority was given to bombers - a decision which cost us dear. The German night fighter arm was hopelessly overstretched.

COVENTRY

In 'The Defence of the United Kingdom,' Basil Collier writes about the German attack on Coventry:

'... On the night of 14/15 November 1940 a new phase of the air war began with the memorable air attack on Coventry. Of 550 German aircraft in action against UK, about 450, led by *Kampfgeschwader 100*, attacked Coventry and in a period of 10 hours dropped 500 tons of high explosive bombs as well as almost 900 containers of incendiary bombs. The bomber crews were intended to attack not only Coventry, but to knock out the aircraft industry and its supplier firms by targeted attacks on specific installations; for example, the Standard Motor Company.

Flares lit up the City, but were hardly necessary as bright moonlight clearly illuminated the outlines. Fires broke out, spread, and showed following crews the way. Within an hour of the beginning of the attack, the centre of Coventry was a sea of fire which could be seen for miles.

Under such circumstances the city had to withstand a severe trial. The telephone network was the first to be put out of action. Heavy damage to gas and water pipes made it a more difficult task to fight the more than 200 fires which raged in the early hours of the morning. The railway lines from Coventry to Birmingham, Leamington, Rugby, and Nuneaton were put out of action; countless streets were made impassable by rubble, fire and unexploded bombs.

Greatly handicapped by such conditions, the workmen of the City services, strengthened at sunrise by reinforcements brought to the City outskirts during the night, earned high praise for their efforts in this scene of horror and destruction, the scale of which hardly anybody could have imagined before the raid. It is estimated that 550 people were killed and 860 severely injured during this night. How many of them, and of the slightly injured, owed their lives to anonymous rescuers, who pulled them out of shattered or burning buildings and brought them to safety, is not known...'

From a BBC report:

'... A pall of smoke lay over the City as men and women crept out of their cellars, looked for their friends and became aware of the destruction of their City. Coventry was unrecognizable.

The remains of shattered brick walls towered like drunken sentries above a scene of general chaos. Hardly a building had remained intact. It was impossible to see where the main streets, which we had known so well, had been. In every direction fires were still raging, and, from time to time, we heard the crash of falling roofs or of a wall.

Until that night, we were shaken to hear that this or that building had been hit. On this Friday, we were surprised to hear of a building which had remained undamaged.

As we walked through the devastated streets, we hardly knew what to do. With all our houses and shops and most of our magical old City in ruins everything seemed hopeless to us. It was as if we were out of our senses.

The Provost, Rev. R.T. Howard:

'... Towards eight o'clock the first incendiaries struck the Cathedral. One fell on the roof of the chancel towards the east end; another fell right through the floor beneath the pews at the head of the nave, near the lectern; another struck the roof of the south aisle, above the organ. The bomb on the chancel was smothered with sand and thrown over the battlements. The bomb on the pews was large and took two full buckets of sand before it could be shovelled into a container. The bomb above the organ had done what we most feared - it had fallen through the lead and was blazing on the oak ceiling below. It took a long time to deal with. The lead was hacked open and sand poured through the hole, but the fire had spread out of reach. We stirrup-pumped many buckets of water before the fire ceased blazing. Another shower of incendiaries now fell, penetrating the roof of the Capper's Chapel on the south side and the Smith's Chapel on the north side. These were ulimately subdued. Then another shower of incendiaries fell, four of them appearing to strike the roof of the Girdler's or Children's Chapel above its east end. On the roof, smoke was pouring from three holes and a fire was blazing through. These were tackled by all four of us at once, but with the failing of our supplies of sand, water and physical strength, we were unable to make an impression; the fire gained ground and finally we had to give in.'

A few days after the raid, while the bomber war still raged in England, the survivors of Coventry erected a stone altar in the ruins of the Cathedral with a cross made of charred beams and the inscription: 'Father forgive.'

DRESDEN

Whether Bomber Harris had reservations about carrying out Churchill's order to attack Dresden is not known. The fact is that, in February 1945, there were hardly any German night fighters left (Prinz Wittgenstein had been dead for over a year), anti-aircraft defence was insignificant, there were no military targets. On 13 and 14 February 1945, the baroque "Florence on the Elbe", one of the most beautiful cities in the world, was reduced to rubble and ashes.

In those days Dresden was sheltering a million refugees from the East who were jamming the city with their bags and baggage. After the inferno the number of victims could no longer be established accurately, but the number of dead can not be far short of the numbers killed by the atom bombs on Hiroshima and Nagasaki.

Militarily the bombing of Dresden was senseless. It did not lead to the collapse of the Reich, did not put an end to the staying power of the Germans and went into history as an infringement of International Law. British historians too spoke about a "crime against humanity".

Margret Freyer is the young woman who survived the Inferno of Dresden. Her gruesome memories are recorded in a book, "Dresden 1945 - The Devil's Tinderbox" by the British author Alexander McKee:

"When the sirens sounded again, my friend and I looked at each other, terrified - surely it wasn't possible? Are they coming a second time? I just caught the radio announcer's message: 'Several bomber units are approaching Dresden.' The voice of the announcer was anything but steady. I felt sick - so they were coming a second time. Knees shaking, we went down into the cellar. This time there were forty-one women and one man, Cenci's husband.

I sat next to Cenci on a box while a non-stop hail of bombs seemed to last an eternity. The walls shook, the ground shook, the light went out, and our heavy iron front door was forced open by the blast. In this cellar now, were the same scenes as had occurred before in the Ferdinandstrasse cellar: a crowd of crying, screaming or praying women, throwing themselves on top of each other. Cenci and I tried to disentangle them and calm them down. We longed for the 'All Clear', but it never came - the sirens had stopped working. But eventually the earth stopped shaking, and now we believed it was really all over. Cenci and I exchanged a glance of thankfulness. Our cellar had held.

Out of here - nothing but out! Three women went up the stairs in front of us, only to come down again, wringing their hands. 'We can't get out of here! Everything outside is burning!' they cried. Cenci and I went up to make sure. It was true.

Then we tried the 'emergency exit' which had been installed in each cellar, so that people could move from one cellar to the other. But here we met only thick smoke which made it impossible to breathe.

So we went upstairs. The back door, which opened on to the back yard and was made partly of glass, was completely on fire. It would have been madness to touch it. And at the front entrance, flames a metre and a half high came licking at short intervals into the hall.

In spite of this, it was clear we could not stay in the building unless we wanted to suffocate. So we went downstairs again and picked up our suitcases. I put two handfuls of handkerchiefs into a water tub and stuffed them soaking into my coat pocket. They probably saved my life later on.

But as we went up the stairs out of the cellar, Cenci's husband came up and said: 'Cenci, please stay here, you must help my sister. She's ill.'

I made a last attempt to convince everyone in the cellar to leave, because they would suffocate if they did not; but they didn't want to. And so I left alone - and all the people in that cellar suffocated. Most died down there, but three women were found outside the door, amongst them Cenci. I cried bitterly when I found out that I was the only one who had escaped from that cellar.

I stood by the entrance until no flames came licking in, then I quickly slipped through and out into the street. I had my suitcase in one hand and was wearing a white fur coat which by now was anything but white. I also wore boots and long trousers. Those boots had been a lucky choice, it turned out.

Because of flying sparks and the fire-storm I couldn't see anything at first. A witches' cauldron was waiting for me out there: no street, only rubble nearly a metre high; glass, girders, stones, craters. I tried to get rid of the sparks by constantly patting them off my coat. It was useless. I stopped doing it, stumbled, and someone behind me called out: 'Take your coat off, it's started to burn.' In the pervading extreme heat I hadn't even noticed. I took off the coat and dropped it.

Next to me a woman was screaming continually: 'My den's burning down, my den's burning down,' and dancing in the street. As I go on I can still hear her screaming but I don't see her again. I run, I stumble, anywhere. I don't even know where I am any more, I've lost all sense of direction because all I can see is three steps ahead.

Suddenly I fall into a big hole - a bomb crater about six metres wide and two metres deep, and I end up down there lying on top of three women. I shake them by their clothes and start to scream at them, telling them they must get out of here - but they don't move any more. I believe I was severely shocked by this incident; I seem to have lost all emotional feeling. Quickly, I climbed across the women, pulled my suitcase after me, and crawled on all fours out of the crater.

To my left I suddenly see a woman. I can see her to this day and shall never forget it. She carries a bundle in her arms. It is a baby. She runs, she falls and the child flies in an arc into the fire. It's only my eyes which take this in; I myself feel nothing. The woman remains lying on the ground, completely still. Why? What for? I don't know, I just stumble on. The fire storm is incredible, there are cries for help and screams from somewhere but all around is one single inferno. I hold another wet handkerchief in front of my mouth, my hands and my face are burning; it feels as if the skin is hanging down in strips.

On my right I see a big burnt out shop where lots of people are standing. I join them, but think: 'No, I can't stay here either, this place is completely surrounded by fire.' I leave all these people behind and stumble on. Where to? No idea! But every time towards those places where it is dark, in case there is no fire there. I have no conception of what the street actually looked like. But it is especially from those dark patches that the people come who wring their hands and cry the same thing over and over again: 'You can't carry on there, we've just come from there, everything is burning there!' Wherever and to whomsoever I turn, I always get that same answer.

In front of me is something that might be a street, filled with a hellish rain of sparks which look like enormous rings of fire when they hit the ground. I have no choice. I must go through. I press another wet handkerchief to my mouth and almost get through, but I fall and am convinced that I cannot go on. It's hot. Hot! My hands are burning like fire. I just drop my suitcase, I am past caring and too weak. At least there's nothing to lug around with me any more.

I stumbled on towards where it was dark. Suddenly, I saw people again, right in front of me. They scream and gesticulate with their hands, and then - to my utter horror and amazement - I see how one after the other they seem to let themselves drop to the ground. I had a feeling that they were being shot, but my mind could not really understand what was really happening. Today I know that these unfortunate people were the victims of lack of oxygen. They fainted and then burnt to cinders, I fall then, stumbling over a fallen woman and as I lie right next to her I see how her clothes are burning away. Insane fear grips me and from then on I repeat one simple sentence to myself continuously: 'I don't want to burn to death - no, no burning - I don't want to burn!' Once more I fall down and feel that I am not going to be able to get up again, but the fear of being burnt pulls me to my feet. Crawling, stumbling, my last handkerchief pressed to my mouth…I do not know how many people I fell over. I knew only one feeling: that I must not burn.

Then my handkerchiefs are finished - it's dreadfully hot - I can't go on and I remain lying on the ground. Suddenly a soldier appears in front of me. I wave and wave again. He comes over to me and I whisper in his ear (my voice has almost gone): 'Please take me with you, I don't want to burn.' But that soldier was much too weak himself to lift me to my feet. He laid my two arms crosswise over my breast and stumbled on across me. I followed him with my eyes until he disappeared somewhere in the darkness.

I try once more to get up on my feet but I can only managed to crawl forward on all fours. I can still feel my body I know I'm still alive. Suddenly I'm standing up, but there's something wrong, everything seems so far away and I can't hear or see properly any more. As I found out later, like all the others, I was suffering from lack of oxygen. I must have stumbled forwards roughly ten paces when I all at once inhaled fresh air. There's a breeze! I take another breath, inhale deeply, and my senses clear. In front of me is a broken tree. I know that I have been saved, but am unaware that the park is the Bürgerwiese.

I walk on and discover a car. I'm pleased and decide to spend the night in it. The car is full of suitcases and boxes but I find enough space on the rear seats to squeeze in. Another stroke of good luck for me is that the car's windows are all broken and I have to keep awake putting out the sparks which drifted in. I don't know how long I sat there, when a hand suddenly descended on my shoulder and a man's voice said:'Hello! You must get out of there.' I got such a fright, because obviously someone was determined to force me away from my safe hiding place. I said, with great fear in my voice:'Please, allow me to stay here, I'll give you all the money I've got on me.'(If I think about this now it almost sounds like a joke.) But the answer I got was: 'No, I don't want your money. The car is on fire.'

Good God! I leapt out immediately and could see that indeed all four tyres were burning. I hadn't noticed because of the tremendous heat.

Now I looked at the man and recognized him as the soldier who put my arms across my chest. When I asked him, he confirmed it. Then he started to weep. He continued to stroke my back, mumbling words about bravery, Russian campaign...but this here, this is hell. I don't grasp his meaning and offer him a cigarette.

We walk on a little way and discover two crouching figures. They were two men, one a railway men who was crying because (in the smoke and debris) he could not find the way to his home. The other was a civilian who had escaped from a cellar together with sixty people, but had had to leave his wife and children behind due to some dreadful circumstances. All three men were crying now but I just stood there, incapable of a single tear. It was as if I was watching a film. We spent half the night together, sitting on the ground too exhausted even to carry on a conversation. The continuous explosions didn't bother us, but the hollow cries for help, which came continuously from all directions, were gruesome. Towards 6 o'clock in the morning we parted.

I spent all the daylight hours which followed in the town searching for my fiancé. I looked for him among the dead because hardly any living beings were to be seen anywhere. What I saw is so horrific that I shall hardly be able to describe it. Dead, dead, dead everywhere. Some completely black like charcoal. Others completely untouched, lying as if they were asleep. Women in aprons, women with children sitting in the trams as if they had just nodded off. Many women, many young girls, many small children, soldiers who were only identifiable as such by the metal buckles on their belts, almost all of them naked. Some clinging to each other in groups as if they were clawing at each other.

From some of the debris poked arms, heads, legs, shattered skulls. The static water tanks were filled up to the top with dead human beings, with large pieces of masonry lying on top of that again. Most people looked as if they had been inflated with large yellow and brown stains on their bodies. People whose clothes were still glowing...I think I was incapable of absorbing the meaning of this cruelty any more, for there were also so many little babies, terribly mutilated; and all the people lying so close together that it looked as if someone had put them down there, street by street, deliberately.

I then went through the Grosser Garten and there is one thing I did realise. I was aware that I had constantly to brush hands away from me, hands which belonged to people who wanted me to take them with me, hands which clung to me. But I was much too weak to lift anyone up. My mind took all this in vaguely, as if seen through a veil. In fact, I was in such a state that I did not realise that there was a third attack on Dresden. Late that afternoon I collapsed in the Ostra-Allee, where two men took me to a friend who lived on the outskirts of the city.

I asked for a mirror and did not recognize myself any more. My face was a mass of blisters and so were my hands. My eyes were narrow slits and puffed up, my whole body was covered in little black, pitted marks . I cannot understand to this day how I contracted these marks, because I was wearing a pair of long trousers and a jacket. Perhaps the fire sparks ate their way through my clothing."

So much for the recollections of Margret Freyer, a young woman who survived Dresden.

THE NIGHT OF 21 JANUARY 1944

THE BRITISH VIEW

In his book "The Berlin Raids-RAF Bomber Command Winter 1943/44" Martin Middlebrook writes about the night of 21 January 1944:

"...The favourable weather continued and Harris ordered the bombers out again on the next night - 21/22 January - but he switched targets to Magdeburg. It was the first raid to this city, which was situated sixty miles west of Berlin. To help with the raid, 5 Group was ordered to send twenty-two Lancasters with twelve Mosquitos of 8 Group to carry out a substantial decoy raid on Berlin, a prospect that alarmed the Lancaster crews chosen. The main raid turned out to be a disaster for Bomber Command; Magdeburg was not seriously damaged and fifty five bombers were lost... The German fighters ignored the Berlin diversion.

The actual attack on Magdeburg is remembered for the death of Major Heinrich Prinz zu Sayn-Wittgenstein, the leading night fighter pilot at that time, with eighty-three successes in the West and in Russia. Wittgenstein's radar operator survived to describe how Wittgenstein shot down four bombers on the way to Magdeburg but then was shot down while attacking a fifth. The exact manner which Wittgenstein's aircraft was lost was never established. No British bomber returned to claim him, and some German sources say the famous man was caught by a Mosquito night fighter though no Mosquito claimed him. A fortunate account sent to me from New Zealand probably solves the mystery: Flight Lieutenant Alfred Muggeridge, bomb aimer in a 156 Squadron Lancaster shot down that night near Magdeburg, describes how his aircraft was attacked by a night fighter. On the German's second approach, the Lancaster's rear gunner held his fire until the range was very close. The fighter was seen to be hit and go down.

This more or less coincides with the version of the German radar operator. The rear gunner in the Lancaster was Flight Lieutenant T.R Thomson from Edinburgh.

Since this time Peter Hinchliffe, a translator and author in his own right, has discovered fresh evidence that Wittgenstein may well have fallen victim of a Mosquito nightfighter - as it had at first been supposed. Peter is reserving the publication of this new evidence until it can be substantiated.

BOMBER COMMAND

What led to the systematic bomber operations against the German civilian population? Professor F.A. Lindemann, later Lord Cherwell, a close adviser to Churchill, wrote to the latter on 30 March 1942 and said that he had established statistically that every heavy bomber could make 4000 to 8000 of the enemy homeless. If residential areas were bombed exclusively, a third of all Germans would be without a home of their own by the middle of 1943. By the same token, Churchill declared before the House of Commons, in May 1943, that it would be more expedient to destroy residential areas than armaments factories.

After 50 years, in May 1992, a memorial statue was erected to Harris, the Commander in Chief of the British Bomber Command. It was interesting to note that he is called 'Bomber' Harris in his home country too. Her Majesty, The Queen Mother, now over 90 years of age, unveiled the statue in the heart of London. The origins of the statue were also controversial in Great Britain and it was not funded by a public appeal, but as a result of a private initiative on the part of ex-service organisations. For the conscience of many Britons had been stirred when it came to honouring the commander whose strategy had [almost] exclusively been directed against the civilian population.

In the United Kingdom too the truth came to light at a relatively late stage. Not until long after the war, for example, did the British learn of the senseless destruction of Dresden at a time when the outcome of the war was practically decided. And so there were noisy protests behind the barriers when the statue was unveiled in May 1992. A banner read: 'Citizens of Dresden, forgive us!' In Dresden itself at the same hour a silent, and therefore even more impressive, memorial service took place.

Had Arthur Harris flown on the operations himself, and had he, having been shot down, landed in the inferno by parachute and been recognized, the people would, presumably, have torn him to pieces. Did he know what happened to his crews? Not infrequently, British airmen who had bailed out were lynched by the enraged populace, without needing Nazi rabble-rousing; on the contrary, the authorities often had to step in, to ensure observance of the conventions of war and protect the lives of British airmen.

Since then anger has given way to sadness. After 50 years it is time for us to understand, to forgive and to forget. Faced with the Harris memorial in the British metropolis, we should not get angry but keep silent.

Let us think for a moment of the crews. How did it look to them? What was their motivation and their morale? The Author thinks, as a former leader of a dive bomber *Gruppe,* he can put himself in their shoes. Had there been crews who turned down these operations, who refused to drop bombs on German cities; crews who deliberately missed the target and dumped their bombs on unpopulated areas; whole crews and individual members of crews who became ill because of the moral dilemma? It would have been understandable - human beings can only take so much.

One reads today that on many a difficult operation a certain percentage of the aircraft involved did not reach their targets. The bomber stream of up to 900 four-engined bombers demanded a high standard of airmanship: coordination of units, precise take-off times, instrument flying, radar control, observing the prescribed speed, courses, altitude, familiarity with alternative landing fields, conduct in emergencies. The long approach flight gave the crews an inkling of what awaited them when they came within range of anti-aircraft fire.

Their nerves would have been tensed to the limit, especially when there was a warning of fighter interceptions. Often a long way off from the target the German night fighters would begin to stalk the bomber stream and, on dark nights, appear from apparently nowhere. As soon as the fighter had reached its firing position it was, as a rule, too late for the British aircraft - the die was cast. So many British airman certainly had to wage an enormous internal as well as external battle to control themselves. The bursting of the heavy Flak, comrades in burning aircraft shot out of the stream, the flashes and fires on impact far below, the blazing cities, a hunch about the fate on the ground of those who have had to bail out - all that will not have left the crews unscathed, however determined they were to beat the Germans down.

On average, one in twenty British aircraft did not return from operations over enemy territory. In the course of the whole war, Bomber Command lost 55,573 aircrew killed. In contrast the German civilian population lost more than ten times as many. In spite of everything the air war did not achieve its strategic goal, the erosion of the morale and the will to resist, however frightful the destruction of German cities.

To introduce that strategy was not the decision of the soldiers, it was only their lot to carry it out. So let us grant the soldiers respect and honour! They did their damned duty.

Fortunately the political discussion on this subject is finished. On the second Sunday in November war victims are officially remembered on the National Day of Mourning, all of them, civilians and soldiers of both sides.

THE VISION

An attempt to understand Wittgenstein, even though he can no longer speak.

"One reason why the speed of the imagination in dreams seems quicker than when we are awake, arises because the intracortically stimulated imagination, in comparison with the series of feelings and pictures communicated by the senses, can run through more quickly. If we just think of the high speed at which the thought processes sometimes operate, or of the even quicker and more lively run of ideas in critical situations, particularly where danger to life is involved, one knows from the accounts of those who were saved at the last moment, that someone who is falling or drowning sees his whole life passing in front of his spiritual eyes. It is possible that we should see this as a partial breakthrough of the dream-consciousness into a waking consciousness paralysed by shock."

Robert Bossard 'The Psychology of Dreams'

21 January 1944: 'Visibility was miserable. Midnight, ice cold, snow clouds.

If the flight mechanic had not been so lynx-eyed, I would have wandered around without getting an enemy in the sights, particularly since ground control radar was considerably disrupted by the aluminium strips known as "window". We three men on board the Ju 88 were thrown back on our own resources. The news from the Command Post was that the bomber stream was approaching the Hanover-Brunswick area and must be flying at an altitude of about 8,000 metres. A complete armada of four-engined bombers was to be expected. But where was the head? Was the given altitude accurate? Were there aircraft already on the home run?

Feldwebel Ostheimer, the wireless operator,

Unteroffizier Matzuleit, the air gunner, and I had already been flying for an hour. Very taut alertness reigned. There, suddenly, faint silhouettes, dark against the moonlit layer of cloud: the British bomber stream. We three were unexpectedly in the middle of it. The hunt began. Now we were of one mind and thought and acted as one man. "Nose", instinct and will to succeed united us.

Within about 40 minutes we had dispatched four burning four-engined bombers into the depths. Now we had to get ourselves into position again. That takes time. Alert minutes, then impatient seconds. I arm the *Schräge Musik* again.

The exhaust flames of the Englishman, the fifth this night, can now be seen clearly. Now we must not get into the eddies but make a clean approach, behave quietly and thoughtfully and not become victims of hunting fever! We get into a firing position again. The 83rd "kill", the fifth of the night is due. The enemy's movements to defend himself will no longer change the situation. However furiously the rear gunner of the Lancaster shoots, the fate of the bomber is sealed. The first burst blows the enemy apart, and bits of the Lancaster's wings fly, to a certain extent, about our ears.

This time no cause for triumph, for at that very moment we ourselves become the hunted. Suddenly a fatal clap of thunder. Fire in the machine. Instruments shot up, an inferno. The aircraft is unflyable. "OUT! OUT!" I shout and jettison the cabin roof. Ostheimer and Matzuleit must save themselves. I am trapped.

Then I feel an almighty blow in the back of my neck which almost knocked me out. Flashes and bright splashes of coloured light dance in front of my burning eyes. However much I try, I cannot see anything I can get hold of. Despite the effort, my mind will not obey me. But my senses are still operating.

The roaring in my ears is unbearable. It feels as if molten metal is flowing through my body. My mouth is utterly dry. I try in vain to shout but am as helpless as an animal wounded in the belly. Is my heart going to give out? Diving into the depths, I try to draw some of the icy airstream into my lungs. That succeeds even if it's painful.

Strange pictures suddenly appear before my inner eye, a kaleidoscope of bright euphoric impressions: a meadow full of flowers, butterflies, a tree in blossom which I can get hold of, then a procession is going by, bells are ringing, a bandsman asks where I come from, a squad of soldiers march past. Then I realise that my brain wants to join in again.

Have I got free now? I am surrounded by the ice cold night. It really is quiet around me. The dark has swallowed my comrades. At this altitude the air is thin, oxygen sparse, breathing difficult. Wait! I can hear Flak shells exploding and see muzzle flashes and fires on the ground.'

> *"All is noise, but not birdsong,*
> *It is the beams, which glow,*
> *It is the windows, which scream,*
> *And they scream red in the enemies' faces,*
> *Who stand outside in the flickering park,*
> *scream 'Fire!'"*

Rainer Maria Rilke

"The way of love and death of Cornet Christoph Rilke"

'Now I am alone with my fate. An agreeable relaxation of body and soul. Saved? A careful collecting of thoughts does good. I hold a conversation with myself. "My comrades! Where are they? Is one of them wounded? We belong together, we are a crew, comrades in war, brothers in arms. What am I without you? We are a communion of souls, a team. - Have I dared too much? - How did you get free? Are you unhurt? I am responsible for you, but I have lost you. My God, I can not bear the separation. But I should pull myself together.'

Agonizing thoughts.

'I must reproach myself about you. I have put your life at risk. Was I entitled to do that? You haven't had things easy with me. I was sparing with kind words. Certainly I often seem stand-offish. At all events, I was incapable of finding the way which makes superiors liked. I am no good at back slapping and chummy talk. I am too self-conscious for that. Perhaps it's the fault of my education. Even when I give myself a shove, I am no good at getting really close to other men. I just find it difficult to make friends. I may be respected, but I do not think I was ever popular. Do I come across to you as proud, arrogant or even heartless? I know you need more human warmth to compensate for the strain on spirit and soul of the daily confrontation with danger.

Am I scared? I have never told you yet. Believe me I am not the tough guy some people would like to make me. Certainly not. I enjoy life just like you do, but I just don't show it. I can't go against my nature. I can't let myself go. I should like to relax. If I only could! I am always catching myself grinding my teeth as I try to cope with the bastard inside me. Whether I want to or not, I get into a sort of rage, a kind of inner pressure.

Waiting to go into action. The telephone is the worst. Waiting-battle-rest-waiting-battle-rest. You know yourself how that eats you up. But I keep telling myself that I must pull myself together in front of you two. I mustn't let my fear infect you. I don't need to show you what fear is. This slinking, corrosive poison which creeps insidiously and treacherously into the soul and tries to turn you round and bamboozle you: 'Don't be foolish! If you step a bit shorter and get out of the way, you'll escape with your young life'. I am often very imperious and seem unapproachable to you. The reason is that you shouldn't notice how things really are with me.

Did you get out alright, men? I have made a lot of mistakes, I was too determined on my objective. But of course you know me and realise what a madman I am when everything's at stake. Forgive me! You've stuck it out with me. I know what people said to you: 'If you fly with him, you won't have time to get old.' I am grateful to you for staying all the same, and I'm proud of you. Of course, you could have left me. There are ways of bypassing danger. Who doesn't know that?! You need time to think it over now. We'll have go on gritting our teeth in this bloody war. Especially now that everything is so hopeless. If it's more than you can take, don't worry about telling me. I'll let you go. You've got to think of your wife and children. It's a bit different for me. I haven't got anyone...

If it wasn't so icy! My hands are painful.

... And my own people? I think of Father who is so seriously ill. And then there's my mother who feels with me on every operation. We don't complain to one another. My mother's a brave woman. My brother's a Grenadier in the land battle; he bears the heaviest burden. Russia, the hopeless distance, the ghastly mud alongside the road, the quagmire, the cruel Russian winter, the icy cold, the storm over the taiga, digging in, in frozen ground. Alex, how do I deserve to sleep in a warm bed while you, louse- and bug-ridden, are in demand without let-up day and night?

> *"Yesterday was a day, so inundated in blood,*
> *So full of wounded and dead,*
> *So deafened by the rattle of MG bursts,*
> *By shell splinters,*
> *And the groans and screams of the wounded,*
> *That I can't write about it yet.*
> *I must first await the end of this frightful*
> *battle, just to see what's left."*

22 August 1941. From, "Wartime letters of students killed in action"

The *Gruppe* without a *Geschwaderkommodore*? Just let me get back on the ground. If I don't just go straight into one of the many fires. I'll train the stiff knees so that they're some good again and can run. I'll know how to sort things out. Until I'm back with my men again, my deputy will lead, as I would wish. I'll organise any car and get myself taken to the nearest Command Post. Tomorrow I'll be sitting in a reserve machine again. I won't be beaten for the top rung among the night fighters.

Flying is my world. In peacetime flying is a feeling of happiness, jubilation, a revelation, a celebration. Looking down from imposing heights on the doings of the little ants, indescribable. One should be modest and humble before the Almighty.

Blind flying is a very precise business: the higher

mathematics of flying. To depend on the instruments without vision is a challenge which we perhaps have in common with the U-boat people. But in action it is all different. The effect of the enemy also comes into play. There's shooting from the ground and the air. You yourself shoot and destroy. There is no room for romanticism. The dreamer is in the wrong place. He who is awake lives longer.

But if fighting is my duty, the battle must be fought decently and fairly, as far as possible. And if I land up on the enemy side of the lines, I'll fight my way through, if I don't break my legs. And if they take me prisoner, I will tell them we shall not give up until we are ordered to lay down our arms. What I will not tell them, is that we too long since recognized the situation and that we are being eaten up by the battle in our own minds.

"It is easy to negate everything and thus give the boot to all that was, and perhaps can still be. But in that case the world is hopelessly sick. A position where you must fight for something you do not believe in, and to feel that this 'must' is a product of reason and not of external compulsion, with the alternative of having to write off Germany as a source of strength and Germany as a sphere of intellectual activity, and then, in such a conflict of opposites, to do your duty not for good or evil, but with unimpeachable composure to the last consequence, this position is the most frightful you can think of. The hours, in which I do not feel the seriousness of this situation on my back, are becoming more rare."

From, 'Wartime letters of students killed in action'

'I have made night fighting, and everything which goes with it, my own. I have learnt carefully and conscienciously to handle a weapon, which is not simple, either from a technical or from a flying point of view. The high demands have stimulated me. I am able to show what I can do.

It is clear to me that war has ceased to be a noble, knightly tournament. If it ever was, only fragments are to be described in the duel under the sky. By contrast the material battle on the ground continues, horrible and dirty, pitiless destruction...bombs transform towns into a blazing inferno with charred bodies by the hundred thousand. I am called upon to defend the people down there and do so with complete dedication and full responsibility, and a clear conscience. Yes, with a clear conscience. But it still worries me. In the machines which I shot down, sat hundreds of British airmen. They did not all reach the ground alive by parachute. Certainly there were many among them who only flew, full of scruples, on operations against German towns, because they had been ordered to do so.

I should like to believe that many experienced an uncomfortable feeling. Who knows whether one or other of them regarded his actions as a frightful injustice and suffered under it. Is it not theoretically possible that, among the Britons I shot down, was a Rainer Maria Rilke, a Hans Christian Andersen or an Antoine de Saint-Exupéry.

Not every flyer is a *homo faber*. There is also the dreamer between sleeping and waking, *homo ludens*. And when I think that such a man, Exupéry himself, pilot and poet, did not return from an operation over the Mediterranean, I am sick at heart.

And, if I meet somebody from the crew of the machine I have just shot down, I shall shake him by the hand. People will tell us that we and the British are cousins. But we don't exactly love each other. Perhaps it is better to say that we love each other with gritted teeth. When I think that I have friends on the Island, indeed, very good friends and that, at the moment, we are trying our best to obliterate each other! How crazy!

When we German night fighters - as recently happened - shoot down 80 four-engined bombers in a single night, and the British know that, it takes something for them to hang about by night again over Germany in spots where the air contains the most iron. Fairness too is not a foreign word to them. And they are brave...

I have often asked myself, how on earth do the British manage to occupy the position they do in the world? Is it sport, fairness? For centuries, the British have successfully pursued the policy of a balance of power. They have fought against the Spanish, the Dutch, the Danes, the French, the Boers and us. They did not always have right on their side. But their prestige did not suffer thereby.

This war will change the world. I believe that the British loss of power will not do Europe any good. The peoples, who are so presumptuous as to claim for themselves the sole right of ruling over others, will sink into misery. They will whirled round and, in the end be impossible to find on the map of the world. Hitler will not see the end of the war. We soldiers shall free ourselves of the tyrant. And when the whole Nazi nightmare is past, and we have licked our wounds, a better future will come. We soldiers on both sides will shake hands. After our bad experiences, we shall put our efforts into making peace.

And the boys who come after us will appreciate and respect what we are doing. They will rebuild this country with us, no matter how badly wrecked and maltreated it has been. They will be able to reproach us with having been politically blind for a long time, but not with having given in. They will be thankful not to have to experience such a war. They will stake everything to preserve the peace and to put a stop to unprincipled politicians.

How cruelly we are killing each other nowadays! Down there the town is burning, the firestorms are raging and sucking people into the inferno. It is our duty as night fighters to be here for the population, and to prevent the enemy bombers from dropping their deadly load. We can do but little, but we are reminded of our duty to protect our fellow countrymen, even if the means are inadequate.

Perhaps one can only love Germany from a distance. The Germans, and I am one of them, tend to destroy again what they have built up, because they have no sense of proportion. Hitler's arrogance, fed by early and misleading successes, disgusted me. In his Command bunker I looked him in the eye when I went to collect my Oak Leaves. A rat in a cage. In was incomprehensible to me how millions of people - me included - could have followed this man.

We soldiers do not make war off our own bat. We carry what the politicians plan: or, we spoon up what the deskbound warriors have cooked up for us.'

'Vice agitates for war, But Virtue battles.'

Vauvenarges

'We soldiers are not born to politicise. That is not consistent with our duty. We do not think of the continuation of politics by other means. We go into battle trusting in the justice of our action. Let someone tell me that, in the middle of a battle, he can evaluate what the political leadership has ordered. We are too close to events to have the same insight as our superiors into the sense or nonsense, and therefore into the right, and wrong, of things. In peace time that sort of thing may still be possible, but not when the Apocalypse is brushing over your head. Discipline is the most pious virtue.

We soldiers entered an Order, whose vow is obedience. One cannot fight the battle half-heartedly. Skill at arms has tough laws. The war made us men. We are no dreamers. However great our successes, we know our limitations and have become more modest. We do not talk to one another about war, let alone about politics. Would we not draw our men into qualms of conscience, if we did politicise? Could we then still demand military dedication unto death?

How clear and self evident it is for us in the front line. The orders are clear. It runs: To prevent enemy attacks by night on our towns. No more and no less.

Now I must think of my lady friend. That is something I have rarely been able to do in the heat of recent months. I would like to declare my love for her. Can I reconcile that with my ghastly business? Am I cauterized against everything which is soft and tender? I need you. My thoughts are with you and I love you.'

Von Langenau is deep among the enemy, but quite alone
Fear has created a space around him
And he keeps in the middle, under his
slowly burning banner.

Rainer Maria Rilke

'The way of love and death of Cornet Christoph Rilke'

'I am 27 years old and still have much in front of me. I still stand on the threshold of my life. I will go on fighting hard, but without hate and a desire for revenge. When the war is over, we soldiers will build a better future. May future generations be spared what our fathers and we have gone through. Everyone of us is a mother's son. Every life is in God's hand. When everything is over, I shall do what I can to ensure that we find our way to one another over the frontiers. It is a marvellous feeling to stand in the midst of life.'

... Local people found the Prinz next morning, his eyes lifeless, not far from the wreckage of his aircraft.

He whom the gods love, dies young.

The erratic boulder near the crash site sought out as a memorial to Prinz Wittgenstein. The Author (left), Friedrich Ostheimer, the wireless operator (right) and Herr Kallmeyer, the local expert (centre).

OTHER TITLES AVAILABLE FROM INDEPENDENT BOOKS

'SPITFIRE ON MY TAIL'

A View From The Other Side

Ulrich Steinhilper & Peter Osborne

Non-fiction, Illustrated, ISBN 1 872836 003

'Spitfire On My Tail' is the detailed account of how one German grew up and joined the *Luftwaffe* as a career officer and airman. It was written by Ulrich Steinhilper who was an *Oberleutnant* with JG 52 (52nd Fighter Wing) based at Coquelles near Calais. He flew over one-hundred and fifty combat missions during the Battle of Britain and saw his *Gruppe* of thirty-six experienced pilots whittled down to just a handful by October 1940. It is a very personal and human story of the naivety of youth being shaped by the forces of war. Poignant lessons learned by tragic accidents, counterbalanced by anger towards those who saw the war as a means of personal advancement. Hardback, 352 pages, 84 illustrations.
Price: £14.95

'TEN MINUTES TO BUFFALO'

The Story of Germany's Great Escaper

Ulrich Steinhilper & Peter Osborne

Non-Fiction, Illustrated, ISBN 1 872836 01 1

'Ten Minutes to Buffalo' is the long-awaited sequel to Ulrich Steinhilper's highly successful first book and is a catalogue of courage and determination on the ground. In this way it is set to repeat the successful formula by providing a rare chance to witness how things were for *'The Other Side,'* this time behind the barbed wire and in Ulrich Steinhilper's case all too often outside the wire! It relates a story of remarkable courage and perseverance in the most terrible conditions, braving arctic weather and appalling hardship with one thought in mind - to get home.

Very little has ever been written about the conditions of German officers as prisoners of the Allies and practically nothing of their ingenuity and perseverance in planning and executing escape plans so similar to their counterparts in German hands. This remarkable book is entirely written from original hand-written sheets which date from 1942 and which give it a great immediacy and accuracy. Hardback, 431 pages, 45 illustrations.
Price: £14.95

ULRICH STEINHILPER PETER OSBORNE

'FULL CIRCLE'

The Long Way Home From Canada

Ulrich Steinhilper & Peter Osborne

Non-Fiction, Illustrated, ISBN 1 872836 02 X

'Full Circle' is the last of three books which record Ulrich Steinhilper's remarkable experiences in the Second World War. From being a front line fighter pilot in the Battle of Britain he becomes a Prisoner of War, but for Ulrich the war is far from over.

In *'Ten Minutes To Buffalo'*, the story of the first three escapes is told and in *'Full Circle'* the story is continued as Ulrich and Hinnerk Waller find themselves back in custody. But that is far from the end of Ulrich's career as an escaper. Locking up large numbers of bright young men led to the most ingenious schemes to manufacture their own radios, make their own tools and later, on their *Ehrenwort* (word of honour), to rebuild and run a farm. Lastly, Ulrich describes in graphic detail his last attempt to get back to Germany, admitting it was the worst mistake he ever made in his life. From documents, hand-written at the time, and from numerous letters and postcards home he accurately reconstructs what it was like to be a prisoner of the Allies and the hardships that brought at the end.

'Full Circle' completes Ulrich Steinhilper's odyssey and with it what is now being described as one of the most important contributions to the broader history of the Second World War to emerge in recent times. Hardback, 408 pages, 74 illustrations.
Price: £14.95

'BORN LEADER'

The Story of Guy Gibson
VC, DFC & Bar, DSO & Bar

Alan Cooper

Non-Fiction, Illustrated, ISBN 1 872836 03 8

There is little doubt that if asked to name a bomber pilot from the Second World War most people would name Guy Gibson. Not only was he an outstanding pilot but he was to lead the famous Dambusters raid on the night of 16th/17th May 1943. Post-war the film of the operation ensured that Gibson became a household name, even though he had been killed in the latter stages of the war.

'Born Leader' is a detailed account of how circumstances moulded one of the most outstanding pilots of our time, written by Alan Cooper who is recognised as being one of the most knowledgable authors on the subject. Hardback, 192 Pages, 44 illustrations. **Price: £14.95**

'BORN LEADER'

SPECIAL EDITION

A special edition of 'Born Leader' is available containing the signatures of at least eight people who either flew on the Dams Raid or were 617 Squadron groundcrew on the night of the raid. Added to this are the signatures of Richard James DFM, who flew with Gibson on night fighters and Richard Todd, who played Gibson in the post-war film of the raid; at least ten signatures in all. A complete list is available by return.

The signed editions are individually numbered and limited to 617 copies. **Priced at £24.95**

Each of the copies of this special edition raises £5.00 for charity and to date over £2000 has already been donated to charities like The RAF Benevolent Fund Eagle Lodge Appeal and the Cheshire Foundation.

NEW FROM INDEPENDENT BOOKS
'PETER FIVE'
Freddie Clark
Non-Fiction, Illustrated, ISBN 1 872836 04 6

This is a completely new and wonderfully well researched account of Freddie Clark's RAF career - from initial training in South Africa, through what he describes as being, *'converted, frustrated, conveyed and converted again,'* to fly modified Halifaxes on the top secret SOE (Special Operations Executive) Operations over occupied France.

More than this *'Peter Five'* has been painstakingly constructed as a chronicle of seventy-five years of RAF history, beginning as it does, with the story of Freddie's relative, Bert Stanley, who began his service in the Great War as a Crossley lorry driver, becoming an F.E.2b air mechanic/gunner and later to be returned to *'Blighty'* to be trained as a pilot. Then, with twenty-three hours and twenty-three minutes as a pilot, he returned to the sky above war-torn France and Belgium to rejoin the air war.

This stark account of the early days of training and flying with the RFC is cleverly contrasted with Freddie's own experience in the Second World War and finally brought up to date, comparing it with today's selection and training curriculum for a modern front line pilot. In all a comprehensive and exceptionally well written treatise on military flying, which should delight any aviation historian or act as a graphic memory jogger for those who were there. Hardback, 288 pages, numerous illustrations. **Price: £14.95**

 Also available is the triple set. Comprising *'Spitfire On My Tail'*, *'Ten Minutes To Buffalo'* and *'Full Circle'*, telling Ulrich Steinhilper's complete story to the time he returned to Germany. Individual books are £14.95 but all three can be bought in a boxed set at a considerable saving and <u>all signed by the author</u> at: £34.95 + £3.50 p&p

We charge £2.00 p&p on all other orders because we use high quality packaging and first class post to ensure your books arrive at your home quickly and in pristine condition.

So let the postman do the walking!

INDEPENDENT BOOKS

3, Leaves Green Crescent, Keston, Bromley, BR2 6DN
or INDEDENDENT BOOKS, FREEPOST, Keston, Kent, BR2 6BR

Tel: 0959 573360

** INTERNATIONAL VISA CARD PURCHASES WELCOME **